Knowing You Are Loved

Other books in this series

Knowing You Are Loved

*Conditioning the Habits
of the Heart*

John Guest

Foreword by Tony Campolo

Baker Books

A Division of Baker Book House Co
Grand Rapids, Michigan 49516

Published by Baker Books
a division of Baker Book House Company
P.O. Box 6287, Grand Rapids, MI 49516–6287

Printed in the United States of America

Library of Congress Cataloging-in-Publication Data

Guest, John, 1936–
    Knowing you are loved : reassurance for changing times / John Guest.
        p.   cm. — (Accelerated growth series)
      ISBN 0-8010-3871-5
    1. God—Love. 2. Spiritual life—Christianity. I. Title. II. Series.
BT 140.G83   1995
231'.6—dc20   94–31512

All Scripture in this volume is from the Revised Standard Version of the Bible, copyright 1946, 1952, 1971, and 1973 by the Division of Christian Education of the National Council of the Churches of Christ in the United States of America.

To my dear "Mum," Hazell,
who loved her children
through some very painful years

Contents

Foreword

On one occasion, some people came to Jesus and asked him to *tell them simply* if he was the messiah. They did not want some complicated, "heavy" explanation. They had no interest in any theological jargon. They had no tolerance for the philosophical double-talk that marks the dissertations of contemporary professional gurus. They wanted the truth—plain and simple. They just wanted to know if the man, Jesus, was the one who could save them from the evils of their world and the troubles of their tortured lives.

In our times, there is still a hunger for simple truth. Everywhere, people are searching for an answer to the riddles of their lives in terms they can grasp. In every sector of human endeavor men and women search for meaning. Unfortunately, when the hungry sheep look up, they usually receive a stone. The stone may be crafted in the eloquence of poetry, or it may be written with the accuracy of logical prose. But, in the end, it is still a stone. It has not met their needs. It has not satisfied their hunger. It has not answered the desperate question: "Is there a God who loves me—personally?"

I spent several years in seminary trying to prepare myself to be a preacher of God's truth. But the more I got into the intricacies of theology, the more I became convinced that the professional religionists had taken his clear truth and made it so complex that only an elite core of their own colleagues could pretend to know what they were talking about. In answer to the simple question posed to Jesus, they have answered, "he is the teleological ground of ultimate paradoxical being, available through existential encounter with the eschatological essence of dialectical history."(No kidding, I actually heard a theologian talk like that!) After a while, I made a simple decision not to believe anybody who made truth complicated. I had come to believe that truth is simple and that intellectual confusion is the work of the devil. I had come to see that if Jesus is anything, he is God's perfect attempt to tell us about himself so simply and so clearly that no one would get confused. The fact that many of us are confused about Jesus is evidence of how much those who have taken it upon themselves to declare his simple message have complicated it.

If Jesus were here in the flesh, he would give those pseudointellectuals a verbal beating. After all, why would he fail to do a repeat performance of his earlier show? Two thousand years ago, when Jesus confronted the scribes and Pharisees, he let them know in no uncertain terms that he had little appreciation for the ways they had complicated the law of Moses and the message of the prophets. Consequently, I am certain that, if he were physically among us today, he would display the same kind of impatience with modern-day scribes and Pharisees.

What I like about John Guest's book is that he keeps it simple. He helps us to see that in the midst of our heartbreak, loneliness, and meaninglessness, there is good news. He lets us know in an unmistakable way that God loves each of us. When we ask for evidence of that love, John tells us that God showed his love for us by coming down from heaven, becoming a human being, and dying for us. That is the kind of evidence of love that anybody can understand. If we ask *why* he had to die for us, John tells us that he died in our place. He goes on to explain that each of us has done things that any judicial review board would consider deserving of punishment. But the good news, claims John, is that by offering himself up for crucifixion, Jesus took the punishment that each of us deserved and made it his own.

Each of us is given the opportunity of accepting or reject-ing this good news, but none of us can claim that it is too complicated to understand.

In this simple book, John makes clear the good news that God loves each of us and has a wonderful plan for our lives.

What should be our response to this wonderful truth about the love of God? Well, that is what the rest of his book is all about. While the good news is simple, John emphati-cally stresses that the expected response is not simplistic. God expects more from those who receive the good news than intellectual agreement with the simple declaration that God loves us. John makes it clear that our response to the love of God is that we should love one another. Ah—there's the rub!

Loving one another is not as simple as accepting the fact that we are loved by God. Fyodor Dostoyevsky, in his clas-sic Russian novel, *The Brothers Karamazov*, has his key character, Ivan, say that loving one's neighbor is the most difficult thing in the world to do. Neighbors, contends Ivan, dump garbage in your yard, give off horrible odors, and are generally unkind. Humanity in the abstract is easy to love, but the guy next door? Now that is a different thing.

But John Guest does not stop with declaring the simple message of God's love. He goes on to show us how that love can be worked out in our everyday relationships with neighbors, with people at work, and hardest of all, with those in our immediate families. Like any good teacher, he uses stories from life to help us discover ways to overcome barriers to loving others. He gives us multiple examples from his own experiences that can help us find ways to over-come bitterness, resentment, and other hindrances to lov-ing relationships. He explains *how* to express love to the hurting people around us. But in the midst of this easy-to-understand guidance, John also points out that there is a mystery to the message of the cross that nobody this side of the twilight zone will be able to explain. He makes us realize that *why* God loves us so much will always be a mystery. And he lets us know that there is a further mystery to the gospel in that the same love that compelled Jesus to die for us can be given to us—*supernaturally*. John helps us grasp the truth that the same Jesus who died on the cross for our sins has been resurrected from the dead and is spiritually present among us. As a matter of fact, he tells us that this resurrected Jesus is as close to us as the air we breathe. He wants each of us to have a person-to-person relationship with this Jesus.

In such a relationship, Jesus can become a personal guide who will require that we obey him. But there is more— much more! To those who are willing to get this close to Jesus, there is given a supernatural gift. It is the capacity to love people with the love of God.

But, enough of this. Get on with reading the book. If I have not made the message clear it's okay because that is what John Guest is going to do for you as you read what he has to say. This book will impress you with its simplicity. But it is in that simplicity that you may find the most profound truth ever known.

Tony Campolo

1

Someone Loves You

I sat silently, my eyes drifting across the magazines on the coffee table, and tried to figure out what to say next.

Across from me sat a young woman. I say "young," though I was not really sure of her age: in her mid- to late-thirties, I guessed from her appearance and the way she was dressed. At the moment she seemed much older. Her eyes were red from crying. In her hands she twisted and tugged at what remained of a Kleenex tissue.

I had met her for the first time that evening. It was the kind of situation that all pastors run across from time to time: a person in need and not knowing where to turn, the friend of a friend of a church member, coming to see the pastor for counseling.

If her present emotional condition made her appear older than she was, it also seemed that she had experienced enough pain and difficulty to fill more than one lifetime. For almost an hour I listened in silence as she poured out to me her experience of the past four or five years of her life.

She and her husband had divorced after a brief, stormy marriage. Later, her ex-husband's brother had assaulted and raped her. She had started legal proceedings against him but had not been able to follow through because of pressure from her family (who didn't want the situation to come to light) and from her brother-in-law, who continued to threaten her with violence.

She had been seeing a psychiatrist for several years on account of the psychological and emotional trauma she had suffered, with no relief in sight. For about three years she had been taking pills prescribed for her by the psychiatrist; the medication kept her in an almost continual state of depression. When she mentioned to friends that she was thinking of taking her life, they put her in touch with me.

Now she was here, in my study at the church, sitting on the couch, aimlessly stirring the long-cold coffee that remained in the bottom of her cup, waiting to hear what I, a minister whom she had never met, might say to her that she hadn't already heard.

The room was still as I prayed silently. After a few moments I leaned forward and said to her, "Do you know what? I have some terrific news for you."

She slowly raised her head and looked across at me. Her eyes showed the startled look of someone who had just heard what she had least expected. She had experienced years of commiseration, but I was the first person to offer her a simple, straightforward statement of hope. She smiled weakly and said, "I could use some good news."

"Well," I said, "here it is. There is someone who loves you. God loves you. And he wants you to *know* that he loves you and that he has a wonderful plan for your life."

Now those of you reading this who have been Christians for any length of time will likely recognize this statement immediately. It is the first of the "Four Spiritual Laws," a simple summary of the gospel message prepared by the organization Campus Crusade for Christ. You may have heard it, as I have, hundreds of times. You may have spoken it any number of times yourself in the course of explaining the gospel to others.

God loves you and has a wonderful plan for your life. It was certainly not the most original statement I could have come up with in trying to respond to this woman's needs. But it was the statement God prompted me to make in those few moments when I turned to him in prayer, and I spoke it with a tremendous God-given conviction that its message, however familiar and old-hat it may have seemed to me, was precisely what this woman most needed to hear.

Indeed, I had not even finished saying it when I could see that my words had struck home. I had barely got out the words, "There is someone who loves you . . ." when her eyes filled with tears and she began to weep, not the kind of anxious, despairing tears she had shed while telling me her tale of woe, but tears of release, almost of joy, as if a great load were being lifted from her.

We spent another hour or so together during which time I explained to her as much as I could about this God who loved her and who, in spite of everything, had a wonderful plan for her life. She took in what I had to say, prayed a prayer of openhearted response to the Lord Jesus, and then left. It was more than a year later that I saw her again, not as a counselor but quite by chance. It was good to see that she had made a significant recovery.

Now there was much about this woman's life that might seem to raise the question whether anyone loved her. But during our brief visit, the simple, awesome truth that *God* loved her penetrated her pain and confusion and depression. She left my office that evening a changed person. Her spirit, her face, her deportment were those of a woman who had "touched the hem" of Jesus' robe, and with that touch, received power to begin again.

You too may be a person in pain. You may be suffering loneliness, loss, or depression. You may be one of the many people in our society who knows the emptiness of wondering whether there is anyone, anywhere, who loves you. There is. This book is designed to help you get to know him, to get to know the love he has for you, and to live in the certainty of that love.

2

If You Are Longing to Be Loved

Beloved, let us love one another; for love is of God, and he who loves is born of God and knows God. He who does not love does not know God; for God is love. In this the love of God was made manifest among us, that God sent his only Son into the world, so that we might live through him. In this is love, not that we loved God but that he loved us and sent his Son to be the expiation for our sins. Beloved, if God so loved us, we also ought to love one another. No man has ever seen God; if we love one another, God abides in us and his love is perfected in us.

By this we know that we abide in him and he in us, because he has given us of his own Spirit. And we have seen and testify that the Father has sent the Son as the Savior of the world. Whoever confesses that Jesus is the Son of God, God abides in him, and he in God. So we know and believe the love God has for us. God is love, and he who abides in love abides in God, and God abides in him. In this is love perfected with us, that we may have confidence for the day of judgment, because as he is so are we in this world. There is no fear in love, but perfect love casts out fear. For fear has to do with punishment, and he who fears is not perfected in love. We love, because he first loved us.

1 John 4:7–19

There was a popular song years ago by Paul McCartney and the rock group Wings that said that "the world still loves a silly love song." Paul McCartney, of course, is one who ought to know. Almost twenty years ago, when he was still a member of the Beatles, he sang a good number of love songs. He sang one with the refrain, "Love, love, love; All you need is love." Now lots of people have been writing and singing silly love songs for years, and you might think that by now folks would have tired of them. But no—people still love a silly love song.

The reason, quite simply, is that people have never stopped longing to be loved. There is something in us that desperately longs to be loved, to know that someone, somewhere, for some reason, in some way, loves us. One of the main points of the Scripture passage I have quoted above from the first letter of John, and one of the main themes of this book is that there *is* someone who loves us. To make it more personal: there is someone who loves you.

The Great Lover not only loves you, but he longs for you to know that he loves you. He longs for you to experience his love. God, the Great Lover, not only loves you deeply and passionately, but he wants you to know and experience his love in your life.

We Can Know for Certain

I have heard people say that we dare not "presume to know for certain" that God loves us. There may be a God, such people say, and he may indeed love us, but we cannot know this for certain, and to say that we can is presumption.

Many "just plain folks," who would not know how to articulate this kind of theological position, still hold to something like it in practice. They are willing to accept the theoretical possibility of a loving God. But they think he would be so far removed from us, so distant from our piddling daily concerns, that any "love" he might have for us could never reach all the way down into our conscious experience.

It makes no sense to say things like that. A "God" who loved us but who was unable to communicate his love to us would hardly be God. A God who "loved" us but who was unwilling to communicate his love to us would hardly be loving.

Think for a moment how we earthly parents relate to our children. We love them, and we go to great lengths to communicate that love. We do not leave our children in the dark as to whether they are loved. We want them to know we love them. That is how it always is with love.

And that is how it is with God. A God who truly was God and who truly was loving would both be able to make his love known and would want to do so. And the Bible assures us that our God is exactly that way. He is not some kind of mystical cosmic admirer, sending us anonymous Valentine's Day cards. He makes his love known to us; he signs the cards "Jesus Christ." So we know and believe the love God has for us.

If we find ourselves failing to know and believe the love God has for us, we can also know that God wants to remedy the situation. He wants to reveal himself to us. He wants to help us come to know and abide in a living experience of his love for us. Why, then, do so many of us find it so hard to experience God's love for us?

Five Standards of Self-Worth

Dr. James Dobson, the well-known Christian psychologist and author, has said that human beings—at least, those human beings who live in our modern American culture—tend to measure the worth of a person according to five standards.

First comes physical attractiveness. What, after all, is the most readily observable feature of a person when we meet

him or her for the first time? Whether or not we even realize it, we instinctively tend toward a favorable initial response to someone who is good-looking. Someone who is
less attractive has a subtle but real obstacle to overcome
in winning our favor.

When you think about it, it is rather foolish to form an
impression about a person based solely on appearance.
Aside from the ability to enhance appearance by good
grooming, a person really has nothing to do with how he or
she looks. And, when you think about it, how an individual
looks really has nothing to do with what kind of person he
or she is. But the fact is that we don't think about it; it is virtually an instinctive response.

The second standard we use in assessing people, Dr. Dobson says, is intelligence. This one tends to function most
often as a disqualifier. That is, people who seem to lack intelligence are almost automatically disqualified from being
accepted as "okay" by other people. The reverse tends to
be true only up to a point: People whose intelligence is
somewhat higher than average may be admired, but those
who stand too high above the crowd are often dismissed as
"eggheads" or assumed to be arrogant.

The third standard is wealth. Have you ever noticed how
people's attitudes toward an individual change when they
discover that the individual is extremely wealthy? All other
considerations go out the window. Our culture worships
money and idolizes material success to such a degree that
a person who possesses wealth is simply assumed to be a
person of worth. You can be dishonest, arrogant, immature,
insufferable, or all of the above, but if you have money you
can find instant acceptance in almost any group.

The fourth standard is athletic prowess. This tends to op-
erate more prominently among younger people and is more
powerful among men than among women by and large. But
our culture worships athletic prowess. From adolescence

through adulthood, if you're an athlete, the world thinks you're tremendous.

The last standard we use in evaluating people, according to Dr. Dobson, is "coolness." We might define "coolness" as the ability to act as though you have everything under control even when you don't. It has to do with being humorous, with wearing the "right" clothes and listening to the "right" music and driving the "right" car, with being "laid back." Cool people are the ones who go through life with the "What, me worry?" facade carefully held in place. Coolness helps cover up for any lack among the preceding four qualities. It is possible not to be good-looking, not to be smart, not to be rich, not to be athletic, and still skate through on sheer coolness.

How Do I Measure Up?

In addition to using these standards to measure the worth of others, we also use them to measure the worth of ourselves. Often this means clinging to them to reassure ourselves that, despite the emptiness that gnaws at us inside, we are really "okay."

We spend hours before the mirror trying to make ourselves beautiful so that we can be acceptable to others—and to ourselves. But this standard makes no more sense when we apply it to ourselves than it does when we apply it to others. Indeed, it may be even more dangerous since most of us are extremely harsh in assessing our own looks. Someone has commented that if you were to interview the world's ten most prominent fashion models, each of them could, on a moment's notice, provide you with a long list of what is "wrong" with them: their eyes are too close together, their ears aren't shaped right, or they weigh too much (or too little). All these self-criticisms from some of the world's most beautiful women!

We can make similar observations about how we use the other four standards to try to reassure ourselves of our value as a person.

We throw ourselves into the pursuit of money, and then when we have it, we spend it on things that will advertise how well off we are, so that everyone—including ourselves—will accept us.

We show off our academic accomplishments, our athletic trophies, our musical abilities, or a dozen and one other things trying to assure others—and reassure ourselves—that we are worthwhile human beings.

And when all else fails, we "go cool." We put on a front and act as though we're "above it all," as though we couldn't care less what others think about us, as though we're beyond feeling emptiness or loneliness or self-doubt—all to cover the fact that we care very much what others think of us.

And none of it works in the end. None of it: not the good looks, not the money, not the brains, not the skill, not the coolness. None of it can fill the emptiness inside. None of it can quite persuade us that we are worthwhile people.

The fact of the matter is that these five standards of self-worth actually can work against our experiencing genuine love. Most people who are extremely attractive are not happy. The same is true of the extremely intelligent, the extremely wealthy, the exceptionally talented.

Why? Because people who possess these qualities never know for sure whether the people who gather around them and fawn over them and applaud them are really interested in them as people, or merely in their external qualities. A beautiful woman doesn't know whether men are drawn to her as a person or whether they simply want to use her. A wealthy man doesn't know if people are attracted to him for who he is or merely for what he has. And so on.

There is a tragic delusion in pursuing these false measures of self-worth. They don't deliver. They don't make us "okay."

The Longing to Be Loved

Only love can fill the emptiness in our heart. Only being loved can reassure us of what we most need and want to be reassured of: that we are lovable. You may think you possess all five of the qualities I have been describing. You may even be right in so thinking. And yet, if you do not know love in your life, if you cannot perceive yourself as a person who can be loved by another, you are missing something essential, and you know it.

This came home to me recently as I was reading an article about some of the children of people on the West Coast who star in our movies and television programs. Goodlooking? Rich? Well-educated? Talented? Cool? They have it all. And do you know what they have been doing? A dismaying number of them have been taking their own lives. In spite of everything they seem to have going for them, they have become so despondent over their lives, over their own worth as human beings, that they have committed suicide.

The consensus of opinion, according to the article I read, is that they were desperately lonely and unsure of themselves. Unsure, in spite of all the indicators, whether they were worthwhile persons. Unsure whether there was anybody that really loved them. In the end, nothing else was able to compensate for that lack.

Do you see yourself anywhere in this picture? Are you one of those who doubts his or her value as a human being, who tries to cover up the inner emptiness with outward signs of worth? Are you one of those who longs to be loved?

What you must understand is that God is not looking for a performance from us, he is looking for a relationship with us.

He has so constituted us that a relationship of personal intimacy is central to our humanity. We can have all five of the qualities mentioned above, but if we lack this central element, we are frustrated at one of the most basic human levels of need. Someone who is lacking in all five qualities, but yet is experiencing such a relationship of intimacy, might be considerably more fulfilled.

It is precisely at this level that Jesus takes the initiative to meet us. He came as a man to be one of us. He calls us "friends." He offers, in the beautiful imagery of Revelation 3:20, to come in and sit with us and dine with us.

The philosopher Pascal said that every person has a God-shaped space in his or her heart. Jesus comes to perfectly fill that emptiness. We are always trying to fill it with other things, but only Jesus will do. Other relationships of human intimacy—husband with wife, parent with child, friend with friend—are valuable and important. But a relationship with God in Christ is paramount.

A Vicious Circle

Tragically, it is often the case that the very people who most need love are among the most difficult people to *give* love to. It is as if their very need for love makes them act in ways that turn others off. Like some children who kick and scream to gain the attention of adults, they make themselves so demanding that it is hard to love them. The tragedy is that they recognize, in some dim way, what is happening, but don't know what to do about it.

I know a young lady who is caught in just this trap. She very much wants to be loved, to be liked, to be accepted by others. But her need is so strong and her past life experience so damaging that the harder she tries to be lovable, the less lovable she makes herself. Instead she alienates people, turns them off, drives them away. And the torture is that she realizes it and can do nothing about it. "What's the matter with me?" is her constant cry.

You may be just this kind of person: searching for acceptance from others and yet by your own actions driving them further away. If so, there is good news in the Scripture for you:

> While we were still weak, at the right time Christ died for the ungodly. Why, one will hardly die for a righteous man— though perhaps for a good man one will dare even to die. But God shows his love for us in that while we were yet sinners Christ died for us.
>
> Romans 5:6–8

It is Jesus Christ who breaks into the vicious cycle of our need for love and our very unlovableness. For while we were unlovable in terms of God's justice . . . while we were still in rebellion against him . . . while we were "spiritual sociopaths," always "turning God off" by our every word and deed . . . while we were yet *sinners*, Paul says, Jesus performed the ultimate act of love on our behalf. Something that you and I would scarcely consider doing even for the most virtuous person we had ever known, Christ did for us when we were at our least virtuous: He died for us, so that the ugliness of our sin might be taken away and that we might come to know his love for us.

Breaking Through the Barriers

Not long ago I went to visit someone who was in the hospital, in an area near a ward for mentally and emotionally disturbed people. As we were talking and praying together, a man who apparently had wandered out of that ward began to proclaim in loud and profane language his utter hatred for Jesus Christ. I wasn't dressed as a minister, and he could not have heard what we were discussing; I can only assume that the presence of the Holy Spirit triggered something in the spirit of this troubled man.

But even as that man stood there cursing and blaspheming the name of Jesus, Jesus himself was there loving him. How much more distasteful, how much more repulsive, how much more unlovable could this man have been? And yet Jesus loved him, at that very moment, just as much as on the day he died for him.

He loves you in just the same way and to just the same degree. No matter how unlovable you believe yourself to be, no matter how many times you have turned God off by what you have thought or said or done, at this very moment, Jesus Christ loves you just as much as he did on the day he died for you.

It is often the case that those who most need love are the least able to receive it. Not only is it hard to give love to them, but it is hard for them to receive it even when it *is* given.

This is most tragically true, for instance, of people who were battered children. There are people who want to reach out to them and love them, but their past experience makes it hard for them to welcome and receive the love that is offered.

Many people experience the same phenomenon at a less intense level. Some past wound has left them calloused. Because of real—or even imagined—hurts in their past, they find it difficult to express intimacy or to accept love and affection from others. They know they need love, may even be desperately longing for it, and yet they find themselves almost reflexively turning away from it, closing off their hearts.

Often it is this inability to receive genuine love that drives people into sexual promiscuity. They are, in effect, trying to use sex as a substitute for love. But it makes a poor replacement. Illicit sex is not intimacy; it is, if anything, a prostitution of intimacy, an attempt to take something that is essentially *giving* in nature and turn it into something that is essentially *taking*.

Or, if not sex, people try to substitute money, power, possessions, or achievements for the love they need so much and want so badly but find so hard to accept. As we saw earlier, we use a variety of standards to measure our worth as human beings, and all of these standards are simply hopeless attempts to substitute for the one true source of human worth: the fact that God himself loves us.

In this is love, John emphasizes in his epistle, *not that we loved God, but that he loved us and sent his Son to be the expiation for our sins.*

Do you see? He has taken the initiative. The source of love, the source of our becoming able to receive love, lies not in ourselves but in him. No matter how calloused we may have become through the hurts from our past, no matter how insensitive to genuine affection we may have made ourselves by nursing old grudges or clinging to old bitternesses, no matter how thoroughly we may think we have encased ourselves in wrong substitutes for genuine intimacy—God is able to break through. By his death on the cross and his rising from the dead, Jesus has shattered the power of loneliness and alienation and pain. He is ready and willing and able to break through all the barriers in our lives and enable us to know deep within ourselves the overwhelming love he has for us.

"Jesus Loves Me"

I want to share with you a letter that came to me. One of the ushers at our church found it in the collection basket and passed it on to me:

Dear John,

I am 35 years old, female, single through separation. I am the mother of four children. I have lost two children. I have lost my home and all my furnishings. I have lost my car. I am not close to my mother or sister or brother or father. I have lost my husband. I have recently moved 3,000 miles from friends. My two children are seldom with me. I work long hours. I am usually very short-tempered with them. I have gained too much weight. My whole self is ugly.

I find very little reason to live my life. If I could, I'd give away every workable part of my body to some needy person just to guarantee my certain death, as life has so little reason for me. I'd give my two beautiful children to someone who prays for a son or daughter.

Everything has been taken from me, everything I've loved or cared about or wanted or worked hard for. I'll die and no one will come to my grave.

I'm alone, but I have one thing: a mustard seed of faith. And it keeps me going, because I hear you talk about reconciliation, harmony, love, faith, and that Jesus loves *me*.

The letter was signed, "From someone who hears what you communicate. I sit there in your church every Sunday that someone gives me a ride."

I found out who that young lady was and got together with her and told her more about Jesus who loved her so much. Because of that tiny mustard seed of faith, in spite of all her misfortune and pain, the love of God was able to break through. Indeed, God was able to help her become capable not only of receiving love but also of giving love to others.

This happened in a most extraordinary way. One day, totally out of the blue, the young woman's father came to see her. He was an alcoholic, and he was dying. Because of the love Jesus had poured into her heart, she was able to love him in spite of the hurt and pain he had caused her, and they were reconciled. She shared with him what she herself had only recently discovered: the overpowering love of God in Jesus Christ.

There, in the hospital in our little suburban town, I baptized the father shortly before he died. And this daughter, who said no one would come to her funeral, hosted the burial of her father who had come to know Jesus and had become a new creation in him. What a testimony to the transforming power of the love of God!

Wedded to Christ

One of the most magnificent images in the New Testament is that of the church as the bride of Christ. The Christian people, all those who are living for Jesus, are corporately described as the bride of Christ.

Some of us may need to extend the truth of that image to ourselves and "marry" our lives to Jesus Christ.

When I started out in the ministry back in England, I used to perform wedding ceremonies using an edition of the *Book of Common Prayer* that dated all the way back to the year 1662. My favorite part of the ceremony came when I would invite the young couple to "repeat after me" the stately words of the ancient wedding vow:

> With my body I thee worship;
> With all my worldly goods I thee endow;
> For richer, for poorer,
> For better, for worse,
> In sickness and in health,
> Until death do us part.

What always struck me as the couple recited these vows was the immense gravity of what was taking place. When most of us hear these lines, we hear only flowery, poetic words. What I heard—and what I hope those young couples heard—was a level of commitment and sacrifice that is really quite astonishing.

Think about it for a moment: to *worship* another with your body, to endow another with everything you have and everything you are, *come what may* (and let's acknowledge that despite the understandable sunny optimism of the wedding day, there is often going to be plenty of "poorer," "worse," and "sickness" to go along with the "richer," the "better," and the "health")! This is no small thing, a promise not to be made lightly.

And yet couples cheerfully made that promise time after time. They stood there at the altar and gave over their whole lives to one another. Why? Because of love. Because of the love each felt for the other and in response to the love each felt coming *from* the other.

It is just the same between us and Jesus. Scripture describes him as the bridegroom wooing us, his bride, calling us to join him at the altar and wed our lives to him. Why? Because of love. Because of the love he has shown us in dying for us and wants us to enjoy fully. Because of the love that stirs in our hearts for him as we come to know his love for us.

He has already stated his part of the vow. He has already given over his body for us in his death on the cross. He has already pledged to us all he has and all he is, come what may: whether we are rich or poor, better or worse, sick or healthy, faithful or unfaithful, loving or resentful. He waits for us to seal the wedding compact by making our vow to him.

Can you imagine what it would be like in the church if the man said his wedding vows, and then, when the time came for the bride to do likewise, she hesitated? If when the minister said, "Repeat after me: 'With my body I thee worship . . .'" there was only silence? Can you imagine how nervous the wedding guests would get? Even worse, can you imagine how anxious the groom would get? *I've pledged my whole life to this woman. I've given it all over to her. Is she going to do the same? What if . . .*

I sometimes think that there is the same kind of anticipation in heaven as God waits for each one of us to respond to his love and pledge our lives to him in return. He has given his love and his life to you. He has so much more in store for you. He awaits only your response to his initiative.

If You Are Longing to Be Loved

If you are longing to be loved, know that the Great Lover is longing even more deeply to love you, to bring you into a sure knowledge of his love. Jesus said, "Behold, I stand at the door and knock; if any one hears my voice and opens the door, I will come in to him and eat with him, and he with me" (Rev. 3:20). We might just as well express it in terms of our wedding imagery: Behold, the bridegroom stands at the altar, pledging his life to you. If you will in turn pledge your life to him, he will gather you to himself and your lives will be wedded together.

Have you made that response? Perhaps you have: then why not do what so many married couples do on their major anniversaries and renew your vows to him now? Perhaps you have not: then why wait any longer? Why prolong the heavenly anxiety a moment more? Perhaps you are not sure: then why not *be* sure? Like the vows spoken by the bride at the altar, it takes only a moment and its effects last forever.

Repeat after me:

Lord Jesus, thank you for the great love you showed in dying on the cross for me.

Thank you that even now you are the Great Lover, eager to break through all my callousness of soul and hardness of heart, and flood my life with your love.

Thank you that you forgive all my sins, even as I now pledge to you to renounce them and, with your help, to do all I can to avoid them in the future.

> *With my body, I thee worship;*
> *With all my worldly goods, I thee endow;*
> *For richer, for poorer,*
> *For better, for worse,*
> *In sickness and in health,*
> *Forever.*
> *Amen.*

3

The Love of God

So far in this book we have talked about the love of God primarily from one angle: We have tried to get it absolutely clear in our minds that God does, in fact, love us. In later chapters we shall look at some of the particular ways in which God's love becomes real in our lives, some of the forms in which it comes into our actual experience.

But first we must talk about the thing itself. What *is* God's love? What is it *like?* We will be much better equipped to understand how the love of God becomes effective in our lives once we have come to a better understanding of what it is. Scripture has a great deal to teach us about this all-important matter.

The Four Loves

We whose native tongue is English are at something of a disadvantage when it comes to talking about love. The reason for this is that we use the same word to refer to a number of different things. To take a simple example: When a man tells his wife that he loves her, he means something much different than when he says that he loves pizza or that he loves watching football games on television. (At least he had *better* mean something different, or his marriage is in deep trouble.)

Other languages recognize that there are different kinds of love and provide different words with which to refer to them. The language in which the New Testament was originally written, a particular form of Greek, had four different words for love.

The first was *storge*. This was the word for "affection" or for "really liking" something. This is the kind of love we are talking about when we say we "love" golf or that we "love" an item of clothing in a catalog.

The second was *phileo*. Most of us recognize this as the root of the word for "brotherly love" *(philadelphia)*, the kind of concern and care that we are to show toward our fellows. It is the kind of love that motivates us to put a few coins into the Salvation Army kettle at Christmastime or, one would hope, to perform even greater acts of kindness. William Penn, the early American settler, made this the name of an entire city, hoping that the residents of that city would always be characterized by this quality.

Next comes *eros*. This word has become somewhat tainted by our modern usage. We tend to use it as a euphemism for "lust." The people who put out pornographic magazines and movies try to tell us that they are producing "erotic art." In fact, however, *eros* refers to something far more noble: the romantic love that exists between a man and a woman. It has a sexual implication, to be sure, but its meaning goes beyond just our sexual instincts and urges.

The fourth Greek word for love is the greatest and most glorious of all: it is *agape*, which describes sacrificial love.

Agape contains nothing of the self-interest that often motivates *storge* (in which we "like" something because it gives us pleasure). It has no element of enlightened self-interest as does *philadelphia* (in which we look out for one another in the half-conscious expectation that someday we, too, might need looking after). It contains none of the emotional (let alone sexual) self-gratification that is part of *eros*. *Agape* is pure selflessness. It loves with no expectation of being loved in return, even with no expectation of being patted on the back for its very selflessness.

Scripture teaches us, as we saw in the previous chapter, that "God is love" (1 John 4:8). The Greek word used in this verse is *agape*. God is utterly selfless, utterly self-giving, utterly self-sacrificing. In fact, he not only possesses these qualities, he actually embodies them. He *is* selflessness. He *is* self-giving-ness. He *is* self-sacrifice. God *is* *agape*.

Love Before the Beginning

Now one of the things we know about love is that it requires an object. We cannot, if you will, "just love." We have to love some*thing* or some*one*.

Some of the questions that people sometimes ask when they begin to think about creation are, "Whatever was God doing before he created us? Was he perfectly alone? If so, how could he love? *Whom* could he love?"

These questions raise a profound truth, one with which we must come to grips if we are to grasp what we are talking about when we talk about the love of God. It has to do with the fact that God is one God, but three persons. In other words, it has to do with the Christian doctrine of the Trinity.

There is probably no element of Christian teaching that is as hard for us to wrap our minds around as the doctrine of the Trinity. I suppose that is because it is so alien to our experience. Everyone we know, after all, is only one person. How can someone be three persons, even if that someone is God?

But the doctrine of the Trinity is the key to answering our question concerning what God was doing before he created the world. He was loving, and he was loving himself, not in the conceited, self-glorifying way that we use the term with regard to ourselves, but in the same way that *agape* always loves. God the Father was eternally loving God the

Son and God the Holy Spirit. God the Son was eternally loving the Father and the Spirit. The Spirit was eternally loving the Father and the Son. And on and on it goes, the ultimate love triangle.

I mention all this, in part, because it helps keep us from saying one of the silly things that people sometimes say about God. I heard it said, in fact, just the other day. I was listening to a talk show on a Christian radio station, and someone was saying that God created us because he was lonely and needed someone to love. They said it in a kind of maudlin, sentimental way: Poor God, all alone, rattling around up there in an empty heaven, feeling sorry for himself because he hadn't anyone to love.

Created Out of Love

From what we have said earlier about the different kinds of love, do you see the problem with this? It makes God's love for us self-serving. It says that God loves us simply to meet some need in himself. That would make his love anything but self-giving and self-sacrificing.

Note how Scripture describes God's crowning creation:

> Then God said, "Let us make man in our image, after our likeness. . . ." So God created man in his own image, in the image of God he created him; male and female he created them. . . . And God saw everything that he had made, and behold, it was very good.
>
> Genesis 1:26, 27, 31

The first thing we notice in this familiar passage of Scripture is that when God speaks in verse 26, it is in the plural. "Let *us* make man in *our* image, after *our* likeness." It is as though we were hearing the transcript of a conversation among the three persons of the Trinity.

The second thing we notice is the recurring phrase, "image and likeness." This does not mean, as we probably used to think when we were children in Sunday school, that God has arms and legs, and hair on his head. It means that we human beings in some way share in God's character and nature. It means, in part, that we are able to love and be loved with the love of the Trinity.

Consider what all this means. We have these three perfect beings, loving one another perfectly, enjoying one another's love in perfect fulfillment, saying, "Let us add to the circle. Let us create more beings capable of sharing in our love, capable of loving and of being loved just as we are." Not because he needed someone to love, but because he wanted more persons to share in his love, not for his sake but for ours.

We find in our own experience a dim and imperfect image of this very thing. Out of their love for one another, husbands and wives begin to want to extend that love by bringing a child into the world. Now of course we have mixed motives. We often have children because we are, in fact, feeling somewhat lonely even in our marriage relationship and because we do "need someone else to love." But usually we also experience something of the same motive that inspired God to create us: *agape* love, the desire to give of ourselves purely for the sake of another.

And so we come to understand the love of God, in part, through the creation. What more loving thing could he have done than create us? Especially to create us to share in his own life of love? To create us in his own image and likeness?

Redeemed Out of Love

But as soon as we say this, we realize that we do not bear the perfect image of God as we did when we were first created. Sin has entered the picture and has marred that image. By our sin and our sinfulness, we have turned our backs on God's love and thus have lost the perfection and beauty that was originally ours.

This brings us to a second way in which we experience and come to understand God's love for us: our redemption. As Paul says,

> While we were still weak, at the right time Christ died for the ungodly. Why, one will hardly die for a righteous man—though perhaps for a good man one will dare even to die. But God shows his love for us in that while we were yet sinners Christ died for us.
>
> Romans 5:6–8

Having created us to be a wonderful expression of his nature and character, God grieved—and still grieves—over the destruction and distortion of a humanity he created out of his own joy and love. And in this passage Paul is at pains to show us what a truly remarkable thing God did to put things right.

Try to imagine, Paul says, what it would take to get you to die on behalf of someone else. We occasionally hear stories about people who have done this very thing: soldiers, for example, who throw themselves on live grenades, thus sacrificing themselves to save the lives of their comrades. The very fact that we consider it so heroic when such things occur demonstrates the point Paul is making: that it is a rare and remarkable thing for us to do. Usually we will do it only for someone about whom we care deeply, someone of whom we think very highly, someone who has been extraordinarily good to us, someone who we think undeniably *deserves* it. *Perhaps for a good man one will dare even to die.*

But Paul points out that this was not exactly the case with us. In view of our sin, our rebellion, our destroying of the image of God, we can hardly think that we *deserved* anything good from God. He had loved us enough to create us, and we had turned our backs on that love.

Yet it was precisely then, while we were still in open rebellion, while our backs were still turned, that God once
again showed the depth of his love for us by sending his
own Son to bring us back. *God shows his love for us in that
while we were yet sinners ("enemies") Christ died for us.*

Love That Suffers

One aspect of this that must be noted is the suffering that
Jesus bore for our sake. "By this we know love," John
writes, "that he laid down his life for us" (1 John 3:16). "For
to this you have been called," writes Peter, speaking of a
love that expresses itself through suffering, "because Christ
also suffered for you" (1 Peter 2:21). When he died for us,
he suffered. His love led directly to suffering.

This should not surprise us, given what we have learned
about *agape*. Love that gives of itself without expectation
of return or reward is going to suffer in a world that is
spoiled by sin. It comes with the territory.

We don't like to hear this, do we? We would rather believe that a life of love—especially a life lived in God's
love—is nothing but joy and pleasure and contentment and
happiness and fulfillment. Now all those things certainly
are there. But pain is there, too. It could not be otherwise.
C. S. Lewis in his book *The Four Loves* (which, by the way,
presents an excellent treatment of the different types of
love we discussed earlier) describes it very aptly and very
movingly:

> There is no safe investment. To love at all is to be vulnera-
> ble. Love anything, and your heart will certainly be wrung
> and possibly be broken. If you want to make sure of keep-
> ing it intact, you must give your heart to no one, not even
> to an animal. Wrap it carefully round with hobbies and lit-
> tle luxuries, avoid all entanglements; lock it up safe in the
> casket or coffin of your selfishness. But in that casket—
> safe, dark, motionless, airless—it will change. It will not be

broken; it will become unbreakable, impenetrable, irredeemable. The alternative to tragedy, or at least to the risk of tragedy, is damnation. The only place outside Heaven where you can be perfectly safe from all the dangers and perturbations of love is Hell. (C. S. Lewis, *The Four Loves* [New York: Harcourt, Brace, & World, Inc., 1960], 169)

We can see Jesus' heart breaking on the cross when he cries out, "My God, my God, why hast thou forsaken me?" Beyond even the physical suffering Jesus endured in being scourged and crucified was the suffering he endured in taking upon himself all the sin of the world and in bearing the penalty for that sin. Jesus—who had never known forsakenness, who had never known alienation from the Father or the Spirit, ever, throughout the whole of eternity—took upon himself all the pain and alienation and loneliness of a world gone mad and suffered the condemnation that *we* rightfully deserved.

Why? Out of love for us, so that we might be redeemed, literally "bought back" out of sin and darkness, and restored to fellowship with God. He didn't suffer just for the sake of suffering but for the sake of our redemption. That was the goal. He loved us enough to create us in the first place, to bring us into the circle of his love. When we rebelled against him, he loved us enough to suffer and die for us, so that we could be brought back into that circle.

Sanctified Out of Love

There is a third way in which the love of God becomes known to us, one that we might not think of quite as readily as the first two. And that is that God *sanctifies* us out of love.

"Sanctify" is a very religious-sounding word, the kind of word that most of us are content to skip over when we read it. It has an almost distasteful ring to it, perhaps because it reminds us of the word "sanctimonious" with its connotation of hypocrisy and phoniness. We are content to let the theologians and pastors deal with it. But when we let ourselves be content with this attitude, we miss out on some of the most marvelous blessings God has in store for us.

When God sanctifies us, he makes us more and more like himself. Having adopted us into his family, he enables us to take on the family likeness, learn the family ways, become a sharer in the family business, blend into the family style.

Redemption is like receiving a new heart, a new internal life principle. This brings with it new longings, new desires, new motivations for living. Instead of living for ourselves and our own pleasure, we begin living for God, to bring him pleasure. As we do, the whole of our being begins to grow into conformity with the new spiritual life within our hearts.

It is like someone restoring an old car: having installed a new engine, he next wants to begin refurbishing the upholstery, bumping out the dents in the fenders, retouching the paint. He wants to take something that has fallen into ugliness and uselessness, and restore it to its original beauty and purpose. That is what God wants to do with us. Having brought us *to* himself, he wants to make us more and more *like* himself. Having redeemed us, he wants to sanctify us.

This includes, of course, dealing with our sins and weaknesses and failings. Not in the original, once-and-for-all sense in which he dealt with them on the cross but in the continuing, day-in-day-out sense of bringing us to maturity.

Love That Disciplines

And this, in turn, involves *discipline*. Now "discipline" is not a terribly popular word. And it is not a word that we immediately associate with love. If God loves us, we think, then why does he want to discipline us? We are just like a little child, looking up at its father through tear-filled eyes and crying, "Why are you spanking me, Daddy? I thought you loved me!"

"Ah, but I *do* love you," says the father. "That is *why* I am spanking you."

It is just the same with God and us. He does not discipline us *in spite of* his love for us, he disciplines us *because of* his love for us. He knows better than we can know the joy and fulfillment that will be ours when we are more conformed to the likeness of Jesus. He loves us enough to want us to know that joy. Our sinful tendencies, our weaknesses, our imperfections cause him pain not only because they are offensive but because they block our progress toward holiness. He loves us too much to let them remain in our path. And so, out of his great love for us, he disciplines us.

The writer of the letter to the Hebrews uses precisely this same analogy to describe the process by which God works in our life to bring us to holiness:

> Have you forgotten the exhortation which addresses you as sons?—
>
> > "My son, do not regard lightly the discipline of the Lord,
> > nor lose courage when you are punished by him.
> > *For the Lord disciplines him whom he loves*,
> > and chastises every son whom he receives."
>
> It is for discipline that you have to endure. God is treating you as sons; for what son is there whom his father does not discipline? If you are left without discipline, in which all have participated, then you are illegitimate children and not sons. Besides this, we have had earthly fathers to discipline us and we respected them. Shall we not much more be subject to the Father of spirits and live? For they disciplined us for a short time at their pleasure, *but he disciplines us for our good, that we may share his holiness*. For the moment all discipline seems painful rather than pleasant; later it

yields the peaceful fruit of righteousness to those who have been trained by it.

Hebrews 12:5–11, emphasis added

Many parents have been afraid to discipline their children. They have read too many magazine articles by too many "experts" who have warned them of the horrible psychological scars that will result from a physical spanking. And, of course, many parental hearts have been melted by those big, tear-filled eyes that gaze up at them and say, "But Daddy, don't you love me?" I have counseled many parents who are too insecure to discipline their children, for fear of losing their love.

I recently read an account of a particular foster child who, because he was so ill-behaved, was constantly being shuttled from one foster home to another. At every home he went to, the foster parents felt sorry for him and were reluctant to punish his miserable behavior because they didn't want to add one more painful experience to his already pain-filled life.

The only problem was that none of them could stand it for long. This young fellow had been in something like twelve different foster homes, and in every one of them he had driven the foster parents crazy in no time flat.

Finally he was placed in a home where the parents understood that love means discipline and were secure enough to exercise it. His behavior was transformed overnight. All along, he had been subconsciously looking for someone who would love him enough to discipline him. His rotten behavior was an attempt to push his foster parents far enough to see whether they cared enough to put him right.

That is how God loves us. He loves us enough to discipline us. Having created us out of love, having redeemed us out of love, he also sanctifies us out of love. Recently I got a phone call from a woman who was in the midst of some very trying circumstances. She recounted her problems to me, and my heart went out to her. Finally, she asked the question that so many of us ask sooner or later: Why me? Why have I been singled out? Why am I the one who has to go through all this difficulty?

It is not, of course, a question of being "singled out." All of us, at one time or another, receive our share of pain and suffering. It may be a broken heart, a broken body, a broken family, a broken career, broken hopes. It does not mean that God "has it in for us."

The key to remember in such times is that God can and will use all the circumstances in our lives, even the trying ones, to help us grow to be more like himself. We must look to God in the midst of such circumstances and let him teach us and shape us through them. For the moment it may, as the writer to the Hebrews noted, seem painful rather than pleasant. But in the end it yields "the peaceful fruit of righteousness" in those who have been trained by it. It is all done in love. *The Lord disciplines him whom he loves.*

Love That Abides

God shows his love for us in creating us. He shows his love for us in redeeming us. He shows his love for us in sanctifying us. Do you see that everything, from start to finish in our lives, is wrapped up in God's love? This is part of what Scripture means when it says that the love of God is *steadfast.*

The steadfastness of God's love for his people is a recurring theme in Scripture, especially in the Old Testament. Consider these lines from Psalm 118:

> O Give thanks to the Lord, for he is good;
>   his steadfast love endures for ever!
> Let Israel say,
>   "His steadfast love endures for ever."
> Let the house of Aaron say,
>   "His steadfast love endures for ever."

Let those who fear the Lord say,
"His steadfast love endures for ever."
Thou art my God, and I will give thanks to thee;
thou art my God, I will extol thee.
O give thanks to the Lord, for he is good;
for his steadfast love endures for ever!

Psalm 118:1–4, 28–29

What a contrast with our human love! We are so fickle. But God's love is not fickle. He doesn't have "mood swings." His love is stable; it's constant; it doesn't vary.

There was a popular song not long ago in which a man talked about his relationship with the woman he loved. Apparently they had been together for quite a few years (the lyrics don't make clear whether or not they were married) and now they saw little point in looking elsewhere. The refrain was, "I'm happy to be stuck with you." That's about as much stability and faithfulness as people can hope for these days. They're stuck with each other. But the fact is that they just as quickly come unglued; the adhesive of their relationship is no more stable than their feelings.

What a contrast to our relationship with God! He *loves* us. His love for us continues day in and day out. He goes on loving us even when we don't love him, even when we rebel against him. We can absolutely count on the fact that he loves us, come what may. Whatever pain we may be experiencing in our lives, whatever loneliness, whatever temptation to be fickle ourselves, God is absolutely constant and faithful in his love toward us. "O give thanks to the Lord, for he is good; for his steadfast love endures forever!"

O Lord our God, Father, Son, and Holy Spirit, we thank you for creating us in your image and likeness so that we might know your love. We thank you for the sacrifice of your Son that we might be brought back into your love. We thank you that even now you continue to love us by disciplining us in order to make us pure and spotless and holy. And we thank you that your love never wavers but that you are utterly faithful and steadfast in your love toward us. Help us both to receive your love and to share it with others.

4

The Power of Love

Our focus of attention in this book is the love of God for us. In the opening chapters we concentrated on the fact that God does in fact love every single one of us. In the last chapter we began to take a look at precisely what the love of God is in and of itself. In the remaining chapters we will look at some of the ways God's love becomes real and expresses itself in our lives.

But before we go on, we cannot help but pause for a brief look at how *we* are to show love toward God and toward other people. The fact that God loves us is, of course, the preeminent truth. But God's love for us is meant to result in *our* reflecting a more godly love as well. It would be strange indeed if we were to claim to know the love God has for us without at the same time becoming more loving people ourselves. After all, is this not how love works even on the purely human plane? When we are loved, we become more loving.

No doubt you have seen the phenomenon occur. There is someone who, in one way or another, has always seemed cold or indifferent, barely capable of expressing warmth and affection toward others. Then suddenly they find themselves in a situation where another person loves them, and they themselves are transformed. Perhaps they were insecure before, and the experience of being loved gives them new confidence. Perhaps they were arrogant and aloof before, and receiving love breaks down their aloofness. Whatever the particular circumstances, the basic principle is the same: As we grow in the ability to receive love, we simultaneously grow in the capacity to give love.

This is all the more true on the spiritual level. There is nothing that so marvelously releases in us the capacity to love than the experience of God's love for us. This is one way, I believe, of reading the familiar passage from the first letter of John: "We love, because he first loved us" (1 John 4:19). God's love, as it is poured out upon us, releases in us the ability to love.

Before moving on, let us briefly consider some important aspects of love as we experience it.

The Commandment to Love

The first and most important thing we notice about love as it is described in the Bible is that love is a commandment. The most striking statement concerning love comes in the familiar gospel passage:

> One of them, a lawyer, asked him a question, to test him. "Teacher, which is the great commandment in the law?" And he said to him, "You shall love the Lord your God with all your heart, and with all your soul, and with all your mind. This is the great and first commandment. And a second is like it, You shall love your neighbor as yourself. On these two commandments depend all the law and the prophets."
> Matthew 22:35–40

Jesus makes it indisputably clear that love is a commandment, not just a suggestion or a nice idea. Remember that when Jesus, who was a Jew, spoke to the Jews about a "commandment," he was speaking about something very weighty and serious. He was speaking about something that God absolutely required. He takes the point even further when he says that this particular commandment—the commandment to love—is the first and most important of all the commandments. It is the one on which all the others rest.

We will find this commandment puzzling, even downright frustrating, if we approach it with a wrong understanding of what it means to love.

To "love" someone does not mean to "have affectionate feelings toward" that person. It is not a matter of the emotions but of the will. The emotions are involved, of course, as we all well know. But it is the choice, the decision, the act of the will, that the Lord Jesus is addressing.

We do not have to try very long before we realize that it is impossible to *command* a feeling. We might be able to "work up" a certain emotion every so often for a brief time, but to do it consistently is simply not within our capability.

But when the Bible commands us to love, it does not command us to feel a certain way. It commands us to *behave* a certain way. And our behavior is subject to our will. So love, whether for God or for other people, is first of all a decision or choice that we make, and then one we act upon as consistently as possible.

Thus when God commands us to love himself, he is not demanding that we feel a certain way about him. He is not saying, "From now on, whenever you think of me, I insist that you make your knees go wobbly and your heart go pitter-pat."

Nor, when God commands us to love one another, is he commanding us to feel warm and tingly inside. Another way to say it is, we do not necessarily have to like one another, but we do have to love one another. That is, we do not have to find ourselves spontaneously reacting in positive ways to the habits, mannerisms, and personalities of everyone we meet. But we do have to respond to them with honor and respect, in accordance with scriptural standards of caring behavior. (That is one way of defining in practical terms what it means to love someone.) It is only as we reflect on the love of God for us and understand that he loves other people just as much that it becomes possible for us to love even the people we do not "like" all that much.

Love Is Righteous

This brings me to a second point: that genuine love rejoices in the right. Many of you will recognize this as coming from the Bible's most famous passage on love, chapter thirteen of Paul's first letter to the Corinthians. Verse six of this chapter says that love "does not rejoice at wrong, but rejoices in the right." One way to understand this verse is to say that authentic love is founded upon righteousness and, conversely, that it cannot be based on sin.

What a contrast this makes with the secular world's concept of relative morality. The world around us says that the loving thing to do is whatever makes us (or perhaps others) feel better for the moment. "If it feels good, do it."

Scripture, by contrast, says that the loving thing to do is what God has commanded. Consequently, to love means to act in accord with righteousness. Otherwise it is not really love at all.

Let us put it a bit more pointedly. We can never perform an action that is contrary to God's laws and legitimately call it a "loving" action. We can never show genuine love toward one another by means of any thought, word, or deed that is unrighteous. Love is never expressed through sin. *It does not rejoice at wrong, but rejoices in the right.*

The most crucial application of this principle is in the area of sexual morality. I apologize if I seem to be dwelling inordinately on this topic. I am dwelling on it not, I assure you, because I am obsessed with sex, but because the culture in which we live is. We are already strikingly prone to confuse love with lust, and the incessant drumbeat of the entertainment and advertising media, not to mention the influence of the men and women whom we regularly spend time with, only reinforces the tendency.

The application, then, is this: We can never express love through sexual wrongdoing, neither through adultery (sexual intercourse between two people one or both of whom are married to someone else), nor through fornication (sexual intercourse between unmarried persons).

The Bible makes it absolutely clear that sex is reserved for marriage. That is the only context in which sex can rightly be used to express love. Any use of sex apart from that context is illegitimate in God's eyes and thus cannot be an authentic expression of love.

Young women: when your boyfriend tries to entice you into having sex by saying, "If you love me, you'll give in," don't buy it. He's telling you a lie. Men: for you to try to seduce your girlfriend into sex by calling it "love" is a wicked deceit.

Love is never expressed in unrighteousness. Love rejoices in the right—in what is right according to God's standards. Whenever we do wrong, we cannot hope to make it come out right. And we may pay an awful price for our self-deception by hardening our hearts and callousing our sensitivity to genuine love.

Love Serves Others

The third point I would like to make is simply that the love God commands is not self-oriented or self-serving. It puts others ahead of self. It serves their needs first rather than our own. We see glimpses of this in the passage from Paul's letter that we looked at a moment ago:

> Love is patient and kind; love is not jealous or boastful; it is not arrogant or rude. Love does not insist on its own way; it is not irritable or resentful. . . . Love bears all things, believes all things, hopes all things, endures all things.
> 1 Corinthians 13:4–5, 7

Each of these statements illustrates some way in which love puts the needs of the other person first. When we love, we become willing to sacrifice ourselves—not our righteousness or our virtue but our own ego, our own interests—for the sake of the other.

This, of course, is in keeping with the understanding of *agape* love that we discussed in the last chapter. *Agape* is sacrificial love. It surrenders its own needs for the sake of meeting the needs of another. It is the love that we who are followers of Jesus Christ are commanded to exercise toward others.

Again, this stands in stark contrast to the spirit of our age. Modern people are concerned almost exclusively with self-gratification. Everything they do has this end in mind. Of course, if on the way to gratifying my own appetites and meeting my own needs, I also happen to do something that has the effect of gratifying *your* appetites and meeting *your* needs, that is very nice. But let there be no question as to whose interests are running the show!

A friend of mine tells the story of sitting in a restaurant and being unable to help overhearing a conversation at the table behind him. Sitting there were two women. One of them was married and was apparently in the midst of deciding whether or not she ought to have children; she was recounting to her friend some of her thoughts on the matter.

The gist of her thinking was that having a child might be nice, but she wasn't sure whether it would be the thing that would most "fulfill" her at this particular point in her life. Motherhood seemed like it might be "fulfilling," but what if it wasn't? What if after she had the child she discovered that it didn't "fulfill" her that much after all?

Nowhere in the entire conversation was there any mention of anything other than this woman's potential personal satisfaction. My friend was utterly astonished at the selfishness of the woman's attitude. He found himself inwardly rooting that she *wouldn't* have any children, if only to spare

The Power of Love

those children the inevitable misery of growing up with a mother who didn't seem to comprehend anything about the nature of love.

Perhaps my friend was somewhat harsh in his reaction. Perhaps he had simply caught this particular woman on "one of those days" and thus did not get an entirely accurate reading of her. But doesn't the simple, face value of what he heard represent a tendency that is present within all of us to think only of ourselves rather than to put others first? This is exactly the opposite of genuine love. *Agape* puts others first.

Love Is Supernatural

If you have not already arrived at this conclusion on your own, let me draw it for you: This kind of love is supernatural. This kind of sacrificial, self-giving love that the Lord calls us to is not something that we can generate on our own. It is not of human origin. It can only come from God himself.

And in fact it *does* come from God himself. Listen to these reassuring words from Paul's letter to the Romans: "God's love has been poured into our hearts through the Holy Spirit which has been given to us" (Rom. 5:5). Do you grasp what this verse is saying? Note first of all that it speaks of *God's love*. God recognizes that we do not possess within ourselves the ability to love according to his call and actually gives us his own love with which to love others. We don't have to do it with "our" love. We can do it with *his* love.

Note secondly the use of the past tense. "God's love *has been* poured into our hearts through the Holy Spirit which *has been* given to us." It is not something that we have to wait and hope for or talk God into somehow. It has already been done. We are already equipped to love supernaturally. We need not fall short of the high call of *agape* because we have at our disposal God's very own love.

Buy why, then, do we so often fall short? If we have available to us God's very own love, why don't we take better advantage of it? Sometimes it is because we simply choose not to. But sometimes there is another, more subtle reason. Most of the time we simply lose sight of the resource of God's love available to us and thus fail to draw upon it.

I have a small imported car that I use in and around the city. The car has a fifth gear. It is a cruising gear for highway driving that enables the car, once it is up to speed, to travel more efficiently and more economically than staying in fourth gear.

Now as I say, I *have* this gear. It is built into the transmission. It is clearly marked on the gearshift knob. Any time I need it, it is there. All I have to do is use it.

The problem is that often I don't use it. Why not? Well, you know how it is. I am always on the way either *from* some important business or *to* some important business or both, and my mind is elsewhere. Then it dawns on me that the engine is screaming instead of cruising along. I quickly slip into overdrive and put to use what had been available to me all along.

It is the same with God's love. Once we have surrendered our lives to Christ, his Holy Spirit pours God's love into our lives. We have it. It is "built" into us. Any time we need it, it is there; all we have to do is use it. But with one thing or another, we forget about it and it goes unused. So we struggle and become exhausted under the load of loving on our own steam. The answer is to take by faith what God has done for us in pouring his love into our hearts through the Holy Spirit. In Christ we have the power to "shift into fifth."

Love Transforms Hate

As we do this very thing—begin to let the love of God flow through us—we really begin to experience the transforming power of love. I want to mention just three ways in which the power of love transforms our lives.

The first is that love transforms hate. We all know what Jesus has to say about love and hate:

> You have heard that it was said, "You shall love your neighbor and hate your enemy." But I say to you, Love your enemies and pray for those who persecute you, so that you may be sons of your Father who is in heaven; for he makes his sun rise on the evil and on the good, and sends rain on the just and on the unjust. For if you love those who love you, what reward have you? Do not even the tax collectors do the same? And if you salute only your brethren, what more are you doing than others? Do not even the Gentiles do the same? You, therefore, must be perfect, as your heavenly Father is perfect.
>
> Matthew 5:43–48

Jesus knows, of course, that he is calling for the complete reversal of all our natural impulses. What could be more natural than to love our friends and hate those who are out to destroy us (which is the definition of an "enemy")? We are called, however, to love not on the natural plane but on the supernatural. And supernatural love transforms hate.

It's a good thing, too, because hate is poison to our spiritual lives. At one time or another, all of us have at least been tempted to hate someone. Some of us have given in to that temptation all too frequently. I have seen people destroyed by hate. I have seen it wreck their careers, their marriages, their families. They become consumed by it. It comes to dominate their lives.

One of the most insidious aspects of hate is that it causes us to despise ourselves. At first, of course, it can almost feel good. In a perverse way, hate warms the heart. Have you ever given in to feeling really spiteful toward another person and found yourself feeling a sort of cruel satisfaction, as though by your hating them you had somehow paid them back for their wrongs?

The fact is that your hatred has not affected them at all—but it *has* had its effect on you. It has eaten away at you and begun to tear you down on the inside. It has poisoned your mind and heart. And before long, even if only subconsciously at first, something inside you realizes it. You actually begin to hate yourself for what you are doing to yourself by virtue of your hating someone else!

Similarly, hate is a leading cause of depression. We know the symptoms of depression: fatigue, listlessness, emotional paralysis, and the rest of it. But these are only symptoms, not the cause. One of the greatest causes of depression is unresolved resentment toward another person.

It stands to reason that you are going to be psychologically and emotionally depleted if you use up all your psychological and emotional energy hating someone—and then, in turn, poisoning your own spiritual system in the bargain.

People who are depressed are totally encircled by themselves. They worry about their own needs and problems. And hate is one of the strongest fortresses blocking others out and blocking ourselves in. It isolates us. How can we escape this prison?

Jesus gives us the key. "Love your enemies," he says, "and pray for those who persecute you." It is the latter half of that statement that gives us the simple, practical solution. How do we overcome hate? Pray for the people who are troubling us. When we do, we immediately engage the supernatural love that God has "poured into our hearts through the Holy Spirit." We begin to love them with God's love, and before long the hate has given way. Thus does love transform hate.

Love Transforms Romance

Ah, now we're talking. Romance! This is no doubt the section that many of you have been waiting for.

Many married people—and not only those who have been married a long time—find that they reach a point where "the honeymoon is over." Their relationship has stabilized. They have settled into a comfortable pattern with each other. They are happy enough, they guess, but they miss the "fire" that was there in the early stages of their courtship—the thrill of being together, the loving ache in the stomach, the passion. All this talk about *agape* sounds nice, but what they really want is romance.

Well, let me tell you quite simply that it is *through agape* love that romance is reborn. Listen to what Paul says to husbands in his letter to the Ephesians:

> Husbands, love your wives, as Christ loved the church and gave himself up for her . . . that he might present the church to himself in splendor, without spot or wrinkle or any such thing, that she might be holy and without blemish.
>
> Ephesians 5:25, 27

When he says, "Husbands, love your wives," the word for "love" is—you guessed it—*agape. Agape* transforms *eros.* If husbands would love their wives with the kind of sacrificial love with which Jesus loved us—and, of course, if wives would love their husbands the same way—their romantic love would be rekindled dramatically.

I have found this true in my own experience. Kathie and I have been married for over twenty years. We were committed Christians when we married, but that did not make ours a perfect marriage. Knowing Jesus did not remove from our lives the pains and struggles that come as couples seek to adjust to one another. Nor have we missed the long plateaus when there is little fire and life together is taken for granted. What rekindles our romantic love is to come afresh to the Lord Jesus and under the influence of his *agape* love surrender to one another again.

Too many marriages are lost today because when the going gets tough, couples give up. They suddenly become aware that in the midst of their conflict or familiarity, their feelings of romantic love toward one another have waned. From this they simply conclude, "We don't love each other anymore." But genuine love is more than feelings. It is based, as we have seen, in a decision. This is where *agape* can do what *eros* cannot: bear down and stick it out through hard times. *Agape* thus becomes the basis, the foundation, for a committed romantic relationship.

Love Transforms Fear

Have you ever noticed what an apprehensive society we live in? We are constantly worrying about something. Many of us wouldn't know what in the world to do with ourselves if we didn't have something to fret about. I am convinced that this is a key reason why so many of us are "news junkies," switching on the car radio every chance we get. We need something new to get anxious about. Even if it is only at some subconscious, subliminal level, fear is the ambience in which we move.

But listen to what John says in his first letter:

> Whoever confesses that Jesus is the Son of God, God abides in him, and he in God. So we know and believe the love God has for us. God is love, and he who abides in love abides in God, and God abides in him. In this is love perfected with us, that we may have confidence for the day of judgment, because as he is so are we in this world. There is no fear in love, but perfect love casts out fear.
>
> 1 John 4:15–18

Where there is love, John says, there is no fear. None of the gnawing, restless anxiety that grips so many of us so much of the time. Why not? Because love casts it out.

Or, more precisely, because *perfect* love casts it out. Where does perfect love come from? Not from another human being. Only from God himself. We live in confidence, John says, when God's love is perfected in us, when we come to abide in his love, when we reach the point where we *know and believe* the love God has for *us*. It is precisely here, of course, that so many of us run aground. We have heard of the love of God. In an intellectual sort of way, we acknowledge it. But deep in our hearts we have not yet come to *know and believe* the love God has for *us*.

That is what the rest of this book is all about: trying to make clear to our minds as well as to our hearts that God loves us, trying to make plain the various ways in which God manifests that love toward us. Trying, in other words, to help you know and believe the love God has for you. So if you find yourself immobilized by fear or desiring to see the romance restored to your marriage or wanting to climb out of a black hole of hate that you have been digging yourself into or wanting to experience the transforming power of love in any of the other ways in which I have been describing it—read on.

5

A New You

From now on, therefore, we regard no one from a human point of view; even though we once regarded Christ from a human point of view, we regard him thus no longer. Therefore, if any one is in Christ, he is a new creation; the old has passed away, behold, the new has come. All this is from God, who through Christ reconciled us to himself and gave us the ministry of reconciliation; that is, in Christ God was reconciling the world to himself, not counting their trespasses against them, and entrusting to us the message of reconciliation. So we are ambassadors for Christ, God making his appeal through us. We beseech you on behalf of Christ, be reconciled to God. For our sake he made him to be sin who knew no sin, so that in him we might become the righteousness of God.

Working together with him, then, we entreat you not to accept the grace of God in vain. For he says,

"At the acceptable time I have listened to you,
and helped you on the day of salvation."

Behold, now is the acceptable time; behold, now is the day of salvation.

2 Corinthians 5:16–6:2

The heart of the Christian message, the heart of the "gospel" or "good news" that Scripture relates to us, is bound up in this passage from the apostle Paul. It is that we can become new—totally, thoroughly, completely new. If anyone is joined to Jesus Christ, Paul says, he or she becomes "a new creation; the old has passed away, behold, the new has come."

More Than "Being Good"

The heart of the Christian message is *not* "Try harder." Do you remember years ago when one of the big rental-car companies used as its advertising slogan, "We Try Harder"? That slogan may work as a summary of a business philosophy, but it does not work at all as a summary of the Christian faith.

It is necessary to emphasize this because so many people have managed to get the wrong impression about Christianity from what they have heard in church on Sundays. They have heard that God wants them to "be good."

Now, of course, God *does* want us to be good. In fact, he wants us to be better than good: he wants us to be perfect. Jesus himself said it quite plainly: "You, therefore, must be perfect, as your heavenly Father is perfect" (Matt. 5:48). The Bible is filled with teaching about how we can please God and thus "be good."

Moreover, we Christians ourselves also want to be good. We love Jesus, after all. We want to be conformed to his image. We want to respond to his call. And so we expend considerable thought and energy trying to realize the vision of holiness he sets before us, trying to "be good."

It is possible, therefore, to attend church and to hear what is read from Scripture, to listen to what is preached from the pulpit, to observe what goes on in people's lives, and to pick up the idea that the foundation of the Christian message is: Be good. Love other people. Be a good scout. Do good deeds. Be a nice person.

Although all those concepts may in some way fit into the Christian life, they are hardly the core of the gospel itself. The core is that "if any one is in Christ, he is a new creation; the old has passed away, behold, the new has come." The core is that in Christ there can be a new you. Not just an improved version of the old you, not just, as we used to say in England, "mutton made up to look like lamb," not just a good cosmetic job at the beautician's, but a *new you*.

Brand New

There is something in the human heart that seems vaguely aware of this possibility of newness, that yearns for it and seeks for it in all the wrong places.

The most common place we look for it is in human relationships. You see it reflected in popular love songs. There was a song out in past years, the refrain of which said, "You make me feel brand new." And another that said, "Lying here in your arms, I'm born again."

I find it ironic that the lyricist used the word "lying," because, whether or not he realized it, that is exactly what he himself was doing. He was lying. Being in the arms of a man or woman, seeking intimacy apart from the kind of committed relationship that God has designed in marriage, will never make you "born again." That's a bold-faced lie. Before long, rather than making you feel "brand new," it will leave you feeling jaded and old and used.

Even romantic relationships that do not involve sexual promiscuity, even those that seem wholesome, will ultimately disappoint us. There is, of course, something about being in love that does make us *feel* brand new. But ultimately it's a counterfeit. Those feelings of "being in love," wonderful though they may be while they last, do not last forever. However much better we may feel for having fallen in love, however much we may seem to be improved by the experience, in the end we are still the same person with the same longing to be *really* born again, *really* made new, still stirring deep within us.

Neither, incidentally, will going to church make us new. Not even if you go every week and sing the hymns loudly and put money in the collection plate. Someone has defined religion as "man reaching out to God." Sounds noble, doesn't it? The only problem is, man's arms aren't long enough to reach that far. What we need is not us reaching out to God, but God reaching out to us.

And that is exactly what we have: God, in the person of Jesus Christ, reaching out to sinful man and making him a new creation. It is not our effort but God's grace that accomplishes it.

"He Became Sin"

And what is the means by which he accomplishes it? "For our sake," Paul says, "he made him to be sin who knew no sin, so that in him we might become the righteousness of God."

Let's restate that verse slightly to help bring out its meaning more clearly. God made Jesus, who knew no sin, to *be* sin, so that in Jesus you and I might become the righteousness of God.

Do you realize the astonishing truth conveyed in that statement? God did something incredible in Jesus Christ. Jesus was absolutely pure and spotless and without blemish. He had never done anything wrong. He had never uttered an evil word or entertained an unworthy thought. He had never displeased his Father in the slightest. He had never been distant from his Father. Morally, physically, spiritually, he was absolutely perfect. That is what Paul means when he says that Jesus "knew no sin." God made this utterly perfect Jesus, who knew no sin, to *be* sin for our sake.

Can we get quite clear in our minds what we mean by sin? Christians use the word all the time, and as a result it begins to lose some of its impact. The secular world uses the word, too, but often in a mocking way. Magazines advertise chocolate cakes that are "sinfully rich." Friends jokingly plan to go out on Saturday night and "do a little innocent sinning" together.

But there is nothing innocent or cute about sin. Do you know what sin looks like? I once counseled a woman who had been raped as a teenager. For years she told no one about it, holding inside her the rage and the shame that she felt. Eventually, she married. To her horror, she began to see in her husband's face the face of the man who had raped her. All the emotional turmoil she had bottled up within herself could not be contained. When I met her she was in a psychiatric hospital trying to reassemble the pieces of a life shattered by sin—and not even her own sin, but the sin committed against her.

Sin is children starving to death in Ethiopia. Sin is people being tortured in the Russian gulag. Sin is drunk drivers slaughtering innocent motorists. Sin is a family ripped apart by an alcoholic mother. Sin is a husband methodically poisoning his relationship with his wife by running around on the side with another woman. Sin is the vileness of racism and bigotry. Sin is people abusing one another, lying to one another, taking advantage of one another. Sin is a teenager, his mind clouded by drugs, hanging himself because his life seems meaningless. Sin is selfish ambition, laziness, compromise, bitterness. Sin is even mediocrity.

I am sorry to have to recite a list of such distasteful things. But we can never appreciate what God has done for us in Christ until we open our eyes to the horror of sin.

The Crushing Serpent

Modern man has invested an enormous amount of energy trying to persuade himself that his problem is something other than sin and that the answer therefore lies in

something other than forgiveness. Ever since the age of
the Enlightenment, we have operated under the optimistic
assumption that man can improve and ultimately perfect
himself. As science then began to advance, that optimism
grew. It reached its zenith with the development of the theory of evolution: man, it was held, is inevitably getting better and better. More education, more self-awareness, and
more focused energy would bring us to a salvation of our
own making.

But it hasn't worked that way. All we have done is become
more skillful sinners! All we have done is elevate our capacity to sin and delude ourselves about the true nature of
our problem. Surely our experience in World War II should
convince us of this. The Nazis, after all, who initiated the
war, who planned and carried out the Holocaust of the Jews,
were not morons. They were not remnants of some lost society that had missed out on all the benefits of Enlightenment thinking. Indeed, they had availed themselves of all
that modern culture had to offer. But in the end they were
nothing more than well-educated, highly-cultured, sophisticated sinners.

We run a terrible risk when we try to ignore the reality
of sin or when we try to persuade ourselves that we have
it "under control."

I am reminded of the true story of a circus performer
who for years had made audiences gasp by allowing himself to be enwrapped by a thirty-foot-long boa constrictor.
Now this man *knew* this snake. He had raised it from its infancy. He had carefully trained it over a period of many
years. One particular performance began like all the others. As the man stood there cool and confident, the huge
snake slowly wrapped itself around his body: first the legs,
then the torso, and finally all the way up to his neck. But
then the audience's rapt attention turned to horror. The man
gasped as the snake suddenly began to tighten its grip.

Throughout the circus tent you could hear the bones crack as the snake crushed him to death.

Sin is like that. You may think it cannot harm you. You may think you have it under control. You may think you have it at your disposal, something for your amusement, something you can toy with. But in the end it will crush and kill you. "Then, after desire has conceived, it gives birth to sin; and sin, when it is full-grown, gives birth to death" (James 1:15).

The Rescue Mission

Our great need as human beings is to be delivered from the power of sin that enwraps us. God has perfectly met that need in his Son, Jesus Christ.

"God made him who knew no sin to *be* sin for our sake." At a particular moment in time, God took all the ugliness and filth and degradation of all the sin of the whole world and laid it on the blameless shoulders of his beloved Son.

Let us not leave it at the general level of "the sins of the whole world." At a particular moment in time, God took all the shame and anguish and stain of all the sins of *your life* and laid them upon Jesus. They were obliterated on the cross with him and buried in the tomb with him, "so that in him we might become the righteousness of God."

That means that as we join our lives to Jesus a transaction takes place. All our ugliness and filth is loaded onto him, and all his beauty and purity is given to us. In Jesus we can be washed clean of all the impurity of our sin and be clothed in the glory and splendor of his righteousness. We are re-created. Jesus *becomes* sin for our sake, and we *become* the righteousness of God.

Now do you understand why I was at pains earlier to point out that the heart of the gospel message is not that we should "try harder" to "be good"? Imagine yourself being swept along in the torrents of a river at flood stage. The current is far too strong for you to swim against it. There is nothing for you to cling to, no branch sticking out from shore, no log floating along beside you, no life buoy to be tossed to you. As you are about to go under for the last time, you are carried beneath a bridge. On the bridge stands a fellow who calls out to you, "Try harder, old chap! You can do it! Give it your best shot!"

That is not much of a rescue effort. Simply being urged to "try harder" when you are hopelessly perishing is not "good news." Good news would be somebody jumping into the river, overcoming the current, and pulling you out with him. *That* would be a rescue operation. *That* would be salvation.

And *that* is exactly what God has done for us in Jesus Christ. He himself has plunged into our world of sin and death. He has overcome it by his own death upon the cross and by his rising from the tomb. He is able to reach out to us and grab hold of us and bring us to new life. That is the heart of the gospel: not us reforming ourselves, but God in Christ re-creating us.

The New You

We have spoken of God making us new men and women, giving us a new life. What does this new life look like? Paul outlines some of its main elements in the passage we have been examining.

First of all, we get *a new view of others.* "From now on," Paul says, "we regard no one from a human point of view." What does it mean to regard others from a merely human point of view? It means to see people only through the lens of our own needs and desires, our own preferences and dislikes. It means to value them only insofar as they are of benefit to us and to discard them when we have taken from them what we wanted.

Once we have been re-created in Christ, we are able to regard others from God's point of view. We are able to see them with Jesus' eyes, understand them with Jesus' mind, love them with Jesus' heart.

In practical terms, we arrive at this new way of looking at others through prayer. Is there someone in your life who is making your life miserable? Someone you find it almost impossible to like, let alone love? Most of us have this experience at one time or another. How do we come to love them as Jesus loves them? How do we learn to see them from his point of view? Through prayer. Prayer for ourselves, first of all, that God will open our eyes, soften our hearts, widen our understanding.

But we must also pray for the person we are struggling with. Ask God to pour out his richest blessings on that person. I know all too well how difficult this can be. But I also know how marvelously effective it can be. I have found that it is very difficult to go on despising someone once I have honestly and sincerely prayed for that person.

Second, *we get a new view of ourselves.* This, I believe, is implied in Paul's statement that we become "ambassadors for Christ" who are "working together with him."

An ambassador bears in himself all the dignity and authority and stature of the realm he represents. When I first came to the United States many years ago, I had to go to the American Embassy in London and apply for my visa. There I had to be interviewed by a member of the embassy staff who had complete authority either to grant my request or to deny it. As far as I was concerned, that embassy staff person *was* the United States of America. And she moved with the kind of quiet, confident dignity that showed that she, too, understood the position she held as an ambassador for her country.

It is just the same with us. We here on earth are ambassadors of Christ, bearing all the power and authority and dignity of his kingdom. What a difference this makes in how we view ourselves! We are no longer just ordinary little people, lost in the crowd. We are royal ambassadors of the king of the universe. As the realization of this fact grows within us, we too begin to move with the quiet, confident dignity that comes from understanding the position we hold.

Third, we are given *a new message*. "In Christ God was reconciling the world to himself," Paul says, "and entrusting to us the message of reconciliation" (2 Cor. 5:19). Once we are reconciled to God and become new creations in Christ, we are sent out to announce to others that they too can be reconciled to God and become new.

Isn't it great to have some good news like that to share with others? We live in a society that is addicted to bad news. The next time you're watching television, notice how the anchorman comes on between commercials and tells you he will be back later to fill you in on all the disasters and calamities that have occurred. Bad news sells. It is what we are used to, what we expect; in a perverse sort of way, it is what we look forward to.

I once spent a week preaching a retreat to a group of people who had rented a ski lodge in the Rocky Mountains. We were there for an entire week, sharing God's Word and praying together. We listened to no radio, watched no television, read no newspapers. At the end of the week one of the men who had attended the retreat told me how hard this "media fast" had been for him. "I almost had withdrawal pains," he said. "Back home I am always listening to the news on the radio and television. But you know, it's been wonderful to have had an entire week of nothing but *good* news."

That is the kind of impact we can make on people around us. We can bring good news for a change to friends who desperately need it: news of a God who loves them and desires to wipe away their guilt, alienation, and pain and reconcile them to himself. He desires to make them totally new.

With this new message comes *a new passion for people*. Listen to some of the words Paul uses to express the sense of urgency he feels in sharing his message with the Corinthians: "We *beseech* you," he says in 2 Corinthians 5:20. And in

6:1, "We *entreat* you." A little further on he recounts at length the various hardships and difficulties he has willingly endured in order to minister to them (6:3–10).

Remember that this is *Paul* speaking. Paul, the great apostle of grace, who everywhere insists that man's effort is of no avail and that only the gracious action of God can suffice for us. You might expect that orientation to give Paul a rather aloof view of people, something of a detachment in regard to exerting his own effort on their behalf. But no. We find Paul to be the most passionate, the most on-fire, the most *driven* preacher of the gospel.

God grant that we become as Paul was! If we are to be effective as God's ambassadors, there simply is no place for our ho-hum, matter-of-fact brand of Christianity. Passion for people comes with our new life in Christ. When we are re-created in Jesus, the things that concern Jesus concern us. And nothing concerns Jesus more than the salvation of men and women. Passion for people is part of the standard equipment.

It is tragic that so many of us are regularly in touch with so many people who we know need to hear this good news, but we hang back. We are afraid to bring up the subject. We don't want them to think us odd. And some go along, so cool, so laid-back, so casual, and let one opportunity after another pass us by, until . . .

We must let God stir up in us this passion for people. If we are going to err, let's err on the side of fanaticism for a while. Rather than congratulate ourselves on how good we are at not turning people off, let's see how good we can get at turning people on!

Finally, when we are made new in Christ, we receive *a new servanthood.* "As *servants* of God we commend ourselves in every way," Paul says (2 Cor. 6:4).

A friend of mine recounts an experience he had while riding on a train in England. He was in a train compartment with two other men. One of the men suddenly had a seizure.

It lasted for quite a while and created the need for a considerable amount of assistance which his companion uncomplainingly gave. My friend was impressed with this second man's quiet, earnest dedication to his sick friend and wondered what was at the heart of it.

Later he found out. The two men, it seems, had served together in the army. The first man had heroically saved the life of the second during combat, sustaining in the process an injury that now caused him occasional seizures. "Because he gave himself to rescue me," the second man told my friend, "I have committed myself to look after him for the rest of his life."

The parallel is obvious: Jesus has given himself to rescue us. What could be more fitting than for us to commit ourselves to serve him for the rest of our lives?

God's Idea, Not Ours

"All this," Paul says, speaking of this business of being made new in Christ, "all this is from God, who through Christ reconciled us to himself." New life in Christ is from God. It isn't my idea or the churches' idea; new life in Christ isn't just a religious concept that clever men dreamed up as some kind of psycho-spiritual crutch to help us deal with the guilt and pain and longing for a fresh start that we so pointedly experience.

The passage we are looking at begins, "From now on, therefore, we regard no one from a human point of view; even though we once regarded Christ from a human point of view, we regard him thus no longer." There is a human, earth-bound, tunnel-vision point of view from which men and women in our day look at Jesus. That point of view might be called *subjectivism*, when I decide that only my own self-selected perspective is "true for me." It might be called "relativism" when we decide there is no truth that is true for everyone but that truth is relative to each one's circumstances and preferences. Or it might be called "existentialism" when we tell ourselves that only the present moment and what we decide during it is true. What may have seemed true in the past or what may seem true in the future has no meaning.

This kind of thinking has so pervaded our culture that men and women have simply given up on ever knowing what the truth is about anything. They have lost sight of the notion that there might even *be* such a thing as hard, solid, objective, universal truth.

People hear talk about "new life" or "rebirth in Jesus" and the only thing that comes to their mind is, "How nice. You have decided to believe in something that offers you consolation. That's terrific. Of course, since I don't happen to believe in it, it's not true for me, but it is true for you since you do believe in it. You seem to feel in need of a crutch, and you have found one. That's great. I'm happy for you."

But new life in Christ isn't our idea, it's God's idea. It's a tremendous, overwhelming reality that he wants to make real in the lives of each one of us. God loved the world so much, John tells us in his gospel, that he sent his Son Jesus to live for us and die for us and be raised from the dead for us, so that we might be reborn to new life (see John 3:1–21, esp. v. 16). It wasn't our idea that he do all that, it was his idea, born of his great love for us. We didn't make it up, he made it known to us. And it isn't true because we believe in it, we believe in it because it's true!

Too Good to Be True?

Of course, part of the reason people try to write off Christianity as a mere human invention is precisely because it does meet our human need so perfectly. It seems too good to be true. Anything that fits so neatly must have been fabricated. It must have been invented just to fill all those empty places inside.

But what the critics see as evidence for the prosecution has always seemed to me to be evidence for the defense. What they see as evidence that it all comes from man, I see as evidence that it really does come from God. Does anyone really believe that mere human intelligence could have thought up something as bizarre (in human terms) as a God composed of three persons, one of whom becomes a human being, lives in utter historical obscurity, suffers a savage form of capital punishment for crimes he never committed, rises from the tomb when there is no one there to observe it, and ascends to heaven from which he dispatches the third person of the Godhead so that we might share in his life both now and forever? If *you* were going to invent a philosophical crutch to help you cope with your feelings of emptiness and longing, would you likely have come up with something like *that?*

It was C. S. Lewis who noted that it was the very unbelievability of Christianity that made it so compellingly believable. Reality, he said, is usually odd. It is not neat, not obvious, not what you expect. "Reality, in fact, is usually something you could not have guessed. That is one of the reasons I believe Christianity. It is a religion you could not have guessed. If it offered us just the kind of universe we had always expected, I should feel we were making it up. But, in fact, it is not the sort of thing anyone would have made up. It has just that queer twist about it that real things have" (C. S. Lewis, *Mere Christianity* [New York: Macmillan, 1974], 33).

Besides, why should the fact that Christianity fits the human condition "like a glove" be an argument against its authenticity? Isn't that exactly what we would expect if there really were a God? If that God really were all-knowing, all-loving, all-powerful? If he really were motivated by the desire to meet our deepest, truest needs and reconcile us to himself? But, if God had sent a savior and yet we still had to go unforgiven, then he blew it. If God had tried to bring us eternal life but we still had to suffer eternal death, then he blew it. If God had come to make springs of living water well up inside us but we still were captives to despair and aridity, then he blew it.

But the point is that he didn't blow it. He *did* send us a Savior who *did* pay the penalty for our sins so that we *can* have living water welling up inside us unto life eternal. Christianity's prescription for new life in Jesus perfectly meets the needs of the human condition, which is exactly what we should expect from a God who is intimately aware of and deeply concerned about that condition. As Paul says, "All this is from God."

The Step of Faith

It only remains for us to avail ourselves of the new life God has provided for us. Just knowing about it isn't enough. Even believing in it intellectually isn't enough. Once we have understood what God in Christ has done for us, once we have accepted it as true, we still have one more step to take. We must take a step of faith and hand over our life to Jesus.

Years ago a famous European circus performer named Blondin walked a tightrope across Niagara Falls. Not just once, in fact, but several times: he walked forward, he walked backward, he did somersaults, he did handstands, all on this tightly strung wire suspended hundreds of feet over the falls.

At one point he even pushed a wheelbarrow back and forth across the wire. As he reached one end of the wire, he spoke to a young boy who was standing along the shore watching the performance with wondering eyes.

"You there," Blondin called out. "Do you believe I can push this wheelbarrow back across the wire without falling?"

The boy nodded vigorously.

"Do you believe—I mean really *believe*—that I could carry someone across the wire in this wheelbarrow without dropping him?"

The boy paused slightly but again nodded his head.

"Very well, then," Blondin said with a grin. "Hop in!"

The boy was suddenly nowhere to be seen.

So often we are just like that boy. In our heads we believe the truth of the gospel, but we are not about to surrender our lives to it. In our heads we say, "I believe all those things, and I sure hope it does me some good and that I get to heaven, but I'm not going to hand over control of my life."

Yet there is no other way. The good news of the gospel is not that those who fill their heads with facts about Jesus will be made new. It is that those who join their lives to Jesus, who honor him as Lord of their lives, are made new.

Will you decide, even now, this moment, to surrender control of your life to Jesus? That is what he is waiting for you to do. That is why he has arranged—and you need not doubt that it *is* he who arranged it—for you to be sitting right where you are now, reading this chapter, and coming to a clearer understanding of what God has in store for you.

Why put it off any longer? "Working together with him," Paul says, and I say, "we entreat you not to accept the grace of God in vain. For he says, 'At the acceptable time I have listened to you, and helped you on the day of salvation.'"

Lord Jesus, I thank you for the opportunity to become a new person, to be re-created in you. I thank you that the old can pass away and only the new remain. I thank you for dying for me, for paying the penalty for the wrong that I myself have done. I am sorry for that wrong, and I promise that with your help I will turn from it from this moment onward. Jesus, I surrender myself to you. I place my life in your hands and promise to follow you as my Lord. Thank you for this new beginning, for this moment in which I become a totally new person. Thank you for clothing me in your own holiness and splendor. Amen.

6

Hope for the Brokenhearted

And he came to Nazareth, where he had been brought up; and he went to the synagogue, as his custom was, on the sabbath day. And he stood up to read; and there was given to him the book of the prophet Isaiah. He opened the book and found the place where it was written,

"The Spirit of the Lord is upon me,
because he has anointed me to preach good news to
the poor.
He has sent me to proclaim release to the captives
and recovering of sight to the blind,
to set at liberty those who are oppressed,
to proclaim the acceptable year of the Lord."

And he closed the book, and gave it back to the attendant, and sat down; and the eyes of all in the synagogue were fixed on him. And he began to say to them, "Today this scripture has been fulfilled in your hearing."

Luke 4:16–21

A best-selling book on psychology begins with a statement that is rather unusual for modern self-help books. It says simply, "Life is difficult."

It's true, isn't it? Life is difficult. It is painful.

You cannot read the newspaper and not experience pain unless you are totally insensitive to the sufferings and hardships of other people. You cannot walk along the street where you live or go to your office or go to school without being surrounded by people who are all, to one degree or another, experiencing pain of some kind.

Life is not *all* pain, of course. There are moments of peace and pleasure and joy. But there is also pain. None of us can escape pain, whether it is the pain of others or the pain we feel in our own hearts. Jesus did not escape pain and suffering and neither will we.

So the question is not whether we are going to know pain. The question is whether we are going to face it alone or whether we are going to face it with Jesus. The choice is ours. We can suffer in solitude, or we can know the comfort and consolation of Christ.

The prophecy that Jesus quoted when he stood up to read in the synagogue comes from chapter 61 of the Book of Isaiah. In the original as we have it in our Bibles today, there is an alternate wording that helps bring out the full meaning of the passage. It says, "He has sent me to bind up the brokenhearted" (v. 1).

Why did God send Jesus? Why did he anoint him with the Holy Spirit? In part, to bind up the brokenhearted. To comfort those in pain. To give us the consolation that can come only from God's Spirit.

It is worth noting that he did not come to eliminate all pain, to rescue us from all difficulty and suffering. Rather, he came to be with us in our pain, to go through our difficulty and suffering alongside us.

The fact is that God is able to get through to us in our pain in a way that he does not seem to be able to do in our prosperity. As C. S. Lewis said, "God whispers in our pleasures but shouts in our pains. Pain is his megaphone to rouse a dulled world." It is when our heart is broken that Jesus comes, as Isaiah foretold, to bind us up.

For Love of Shirley

It was a broken heart that brought me to know Jesus.

I was in the English equivalent of high school at the time. I had been dating a girl named Shirley White, who was the most beautiful, desirable girl in town. All the other guys were jealous that she was interested in me.

And she was, too, at least for a while. One day she sent me a letter. It said, "John, I saw you going down the street this morning, and I longed to run after you." And I thought, *Oh, yes, Shirley. Chase me.*

And then, all of a sudden, she dropped me. Just like that.

I was crushed. If you have ever had your heart broken as a lovesick teenager, you will know how I felt. I couldn't eat. I was so distracted I couldn't play sports. Studying was useless; I couldn't concentrate at all. All I could think was *Shirley doesn't love me anymore.*

I tried everything I could think of to get her to notice me again. She had mentioned once that she went to church. As a last resort, I decided I was so desperate to regain her love that I would even be willing to look for her in church. So, the next Sunday, I went.

No Shirley.

I was crushed. But lo and behold, the minister was fantastic. A couple years before, a man with whom I was working had tried to tell me that Jesus loved me, and I had given him a hard time. Now this minister was telling me the very same thing. And this time, in the midst of my brokenheartedness, I had ears to hear. The idea that Jesus loved me reached me. Shirley might not care anymore, but here was someone who did.

"Just As I Am"

I began to go to church more frequently. One Sunday the minister suggested that I join a group that was going to Harringay Arena in London to hear Billy Graham. A bus was going to leave from the church the following evening.

For some reason, I missed the bus that night. I was very disappointed; I really had wanted to hear Billy Graham. It turned out that one of my classmates lived near Harringay Arena. I invited myself to his house for dinner and asked him if he'd like to go with me to hear Billy Graham the next evening. He didn't seem all that excited about it, but he agreed to come with me.

Again I heard from a young American evangelist that Jesus loved me enough to die for me and wanted to give me a new life. I felt more certain than I ever had before that Jesus loved me.

Then he did it. Billy Graham invited anyone who wanted to receive Jesus as their Lord and Savior to "stand up and come forward."

I thought, "He can't be serious! Hasn't he ever been in England before? Doesn't he know what we're like here? This is just Yankee high-pressure salesmanship. No self-respecting Englishman is going to 'stand up and come forward.'"

But to my amazement, a rather large number of people *did* stand up and go forward. As the choir began singing "Just As I Am," I began to get the uncomfortable feeling that *I* should stand up and go forward too. "But I can't," I said to myself. "I mean, I just *couldn't*. I'm an Englishman. We don't do things like that. Besides, everyone would see me. My friend would see me."

By the time the choir reached the second verse, I had stood up and gone forward. And Jesus had healed my broken heart. Not the heart that Shirley had broken, but the heart that had been broken and crushed by my own sin, by my own perversity, by all the filth of my past of which I was, at that moment, so deeply ashamed. I brought it all to Jesus that night, and just as promised, he bound up my broken heart.

The Mush God

It is Jesus who is the fulfillment of Isaiah's prophecy, who comes to comfort those who are afflicted. Jesus himself. Not a theology, not a philosophy, not a psychological counseling technique, but Jesus. *"He himself* bore our sins in his body on the tree," Peter writes. "By his wounds you have been healed" (1 Peter 2:24).

We have a real, live Savior. He walked out of the grave two thousand years ago. He walks now around the United States, Great Britain, Europe, Africa, and the Far East looking for us, searching us out, so that we can come to him and find hope and healing. He is not make-believe. He is not just some ephemeral "life force." He is a person, and he is alive.

He is not that all-too-familiar religious entity that Nicholas Von Hoffman, a syndicated columnist for *The Washington Post,* has so aptly described as "the Mush God":

> The Mush God has no theology to speak of, being a Cream-of-Wheat divinity. The Mush God has no particular credo, no tenets of faith, nothing that would make it difficult for believer and non-believer alike to lower one's head when the temporary chairman tells us that the Reverend Rabbi Father Mufti So-and-So will lead us in an innocuous, harmless prayer.
>
> For this God of Public Occasions is not a jealous god. You can even invoke him at a hookers' convention and he/she/it will not be offended. God of the Rotary, God of the Optimist Club, protector of the buddy system, the Mush God is lord of the secular ritual of the necessary but hypocritical forms and formalities that hush the divisive and the derisive.
>
> The Mush God is a serviceable god whose laws are not chiseled on tablets but written on the sand; open to amendment, qualification, and erasure. This is a god that will compromise with you, make allowances, who will make all wars holy and all peaces hallowed.

A very serviceable god, indeed. But when your heart is broken and your spirit crushed, this nondescript, Cream-of-Wheat god of the buddy system is absolutely useless. You cannot talk to him. He doesn't even know you are there, let alone care that you are in pain.

But Jesus is there. He knows you, knows your pain and struggle and heartache. He is real. And his comfort is real as well.

The Woman at the Well

I have always been moved by the story of Jesus' encounter with the Samaritan woman at the well, recounted in chapter four of John's Gospel. The story is often cited as a model for one-to-one evangelism, as indeed it is. But it is also a beautiful example of Jesus' compassion and comfort.

Weary from traveling, Jesus is sitting alone at Jacob's well near the city of Sychar. It is about midday. A woman comes to the well to draw water.

Already, before even a word is spoken, we know that this woman is an outcast. The custom in those days was for all the women of the village to make their daily trip to the well together early in the morning. As we might say, that is "what nice ladies do." But this woman is not one of the "nice ladies." She comes only after they have gone, and she comes alone.

Moreover, she is a Samaritan. The Samaritans were a sort of half-caste people who followed the true God but were nonetheless looked down on by the Jews. Her first comment to Jesus—"How is it that you, a Jew, ask a drink of me, a woman of Samaria?"—reflects her awareness that she is a second-class citizen.

It does not take long for Jesus to put his finger on her precise point of pain. He asks her to call her husband. She answers, more than a little evasively, that she has none. "True enough," says Jesus, "you do not have a husband: indeed, you have had five husbands already, and the man you are now living with is not your husband."

Here is a woman carrying a heavy load. She is racially and socially outcast and trapped in sexual sin besides. But Jesus looks upon her not with condemnation but with compassion, and he offers to her the springs of living water that well up to eternal life. She came to the well that day crushed in spirit, sordid even in her own eyes. But she drank the water that Jesus gave her and went away a new person.

What has broken *your* heart? A lost love? A shattered dream? A fragmented family?

Some years ago my wife and I had our hearts broken by the loss of a child, a son, who died in the last twenty-four hours before birth. The night I took Kathie to the hospital I tucked our daughters into bed, saying, "Tomorrow morning you will have a new baby brother or sister." That night I learned that the baby had died. When the girls awoke the next morning, I had to give them the tragic news.

That is the most painful thing that has ever happened to me. Where do you go with pain like that? I went to Jesus, who binds up broken hearts. My wife Kathie, herself very ill in the hospital, went to Jesus, who binds up broken hearts.

Where do *you* go when the pain is deep and strong? You can go to Jesus. Whatever it is that has broken your heart, he can bind it up.

Jesus' People

The second great feature of God's healing grace is that he gives us not just his Son Jesus but a family of brothers and sisters in Christ who can support us, love us, pray for us, and encourage us. It is not just "me and Jesus." That is where it begins, but it goes further. It is also "me and all Jesus' people."

Joining our lives to Jesus is always meant to include joining our lives to his people. When we are adopted as his son
or daughter, we come into relationship not only with our
new Father and with Jesus our brother but with all the other
adopted children.

Nor is this meant to be merely a "spiritual reality" (in the
sense in which we so often misuse the term: something that
we talk about but don't really think is there, rather like the
story of the emperor's new clothes). It is meant to be an actual part of our lived experience. That is how it happened
in the very beginning:

> And they devoted themselves to the apostles' teaching and
> fellowship, to the breaking of bread and the prayers.... And
> all who believed were together and had all things in com-
> mon; and they sold their possessions and goods and dis-
> tributed them to all, as any had need. And day by day, at-
> tending the temple together and breaking bread in their
> homes, they partook of food with glad and generous hearts,
> praising God and having favor with all the people.
>
> Acts 2:42, 44–47

This passage directly follows the account of 3,000 new
believers being added to the church on Pentecost. The
meaning is clear: Our incorporation into Christ includes incorporation into the people of Christ. *All who believed were
together.* So it is to be with us. We don't just join our lives
to Jesus. We are also joined to a fellowship of believers so
that when our hearts are aching and breaking there are others who can come alongside us and bless us.

Rejoice with Those Who Rejoice

This is not merely implied in the New Testament, it is explicitly taught. "Rejoice with those who rejoice," Paul wrote
to the Romans, and "weep with those who weep" (Rom.
12:15).

Rejoice with those who rejoice. Isn't it miserable when you've got something to rejoice about and there's no one to share it with? It almost takes the joy out of our rejoicing.

And nobody knows about rejoicing like those of us who know Jesus. We really have something to rejoice about! That night when I gave my life to Jesus at the Billy Graham rally, I left Harringay Arena and danced through the streets of London. I hung from shop signs and swung on lampposts like Gene Kelly in *Singin' in the Rain.* (Well, maybe not exactly like him but almost.) I had the joy of salvation, of being made new.

And since that night I've had the joy of watching many other men and women come and give their lives to Christ and know the same joy that I felt that night. The angels rejoice, too. Just as the whole family rejoices when a mother gives birth to a new baby, so the whole family of God shares the joy when someone first comes to know Jesus.

But there is another side to Paul's instruction. *Weep with those who weep.* Or, as he put it in his letter to the Galatians, "Bear one another's burdens, and so fulfill the law of Christ" (Gal. 6:2).

In the secular world, few want to weep with you when you are weeping. Few want to help you bear your burdens. People don't like to be around pain. When you lose your job, you often lose many of what you thought were your friends. When you lose your health, many people don't know how to talk to you anymore. When you lose your marriage, folks begin to drop you from their social circles; you don't "fit in" anymore.

The results of this kind of social ostracism are spiritually disastrous. A true story illustrates the problem. In Germany, after World War II, there was a ward full of orphaned babies. Their parents were dead and there was no one to look after them beyond the minimal details of feeding and changing them. Most significant, as it turned out, there was no one to pick them up, to hold them, to touch them. Do you know what happened? Many of them died. Why? Because no one hugged them or showed them love.

So it is with us in the spiritual and emotional realm. If we are not genuinely in touch with other believers, we begin to die inside. It breaks the heart of God to see even one of his children neglected in this way. That is why he commands us to bear one another's burdens.

Starving Ourselves to Death

Now there are two ways to respond to this truth. One flows from self-pity. It is the response that looks around in anger and says, "Why isn't anyone reaching out to me? After all, I'm lonely. I'm hurting. These people are falling down on the job."

Do you see that this kind of response inevitably leads us on a downward spiral? Our inward focus ends up cutting us off from any possibility of other people even being able to reach us.

The better response is to look around with compassion and say, "Who is it that God wants me to reach out to and care for?" This is another area in which we are blessed more in giving than in seeking to receive.

I have the suspicion that most of us take the first response most of the time and, as a result, end up missing out on the fellowship and support that is actually available to us. One of the main reasons we limp along in the Christian family with a broken heart is that no one knows about our pain because we don't share it. We'd rather fake it, cover up, keep smiling and acting as though everything is perfect, when all the while we are dying inside. It is up to us to be real with one another, to share our hurts and pain in such a way that we can receive comfort and healing.

The problem—and this is a crucial point—is that we can't just expect to wait until a crisis hits and then suddenly expect to be able to pour out our hearts to those around us.

There needs to be a solid base of relationship on which to place this kind of interpersonal care and concern.

We need to begin *now* to establish the fellowship, the vulnerability, the mutual trust that allows love and care and support to flow freely when the pressure is on. And the initiative must come from us. Don't wait for others to reach out to you. You reach out to them!

One of the most puzzling and frustrating experiences that sometimes comes my way as a pastor is talking to people who suffer from anorexia nervosa. These are people who, because of some complex psychological hang-up, simply will not eat. They are actually starving themselves to death. The problem is not that there is no food available to them; they are surrounded by it. But they will not eat it, even though they can see the harm that is coming to them because of it.

Some of us are spiritual anorexics when it comes to Christian fellowship. We are starving to death in the midst of plenty because we will not take advantage of the opportunities to receive the love and care and support that are available to us.

The Cause of Christ

The first thing that can heal a broken heart is to commit ourselves to Christ himself. The second is to commit ourselves to the family of Christ. And the third is to commit ourselves to the cause of Christ.

One of the things you often hear people say after they have been through a time of grief—the loss of a husband, for example, or some other severe disruption of their life—is, "Well, I've simply got to get on with my life."

And so do we. One of the most damaging conditions that can result from a broken heart is self-pity. It is in some ways even worse because it is harder to get a handle on. The passage of time generally helps heal a broken heart, but it almost always makes self-pity worse.

Self-pity can become a way of life. We get so used to focusing on ourselves that we become consumed with our own needs, wants, hurts, and pains. One of the ways that we can help a broken heart to heal is to turn ourselves outward.

The woman at the well, about whom we spoke earlier, took this approach. Immediately after her conversation with Jesus, John tells us, she "left her water jar, and went away into the city, and said to the people, 'Come, see a man who told me all that I ever did. Can this be the Christ?'" (John 4:28–29).

There is a simple progression here that gives us a recipe for short-circuiting self-pity:

She left her water jar: she put aside the matters that had been the focus of her concern previously.

She went into the city and spoke to the people: she took initiative to face up to her problem rather than continue to hide from it.

"Come, see a man . . .": she committed herself to the concerns of Christ rather than to her own concerns.

In short, she took practical steps to get her gaze off herself and onto the most important thing of all: the gospel. And, lo and behold, it worked! "Many Samaritans from that city believed in him because of the woman's testimony," John tells us (v. 39). Others were motivated by her story to go and see Jesus for themselves, "and many more believed because of his word" (John 4:41).

Reach Out and Touch Someone

The telephone company has for some years now been using the slogan "Reach Out and Touch Someone." That is really a better slogan for the church than for the phone company. There is simply no time to dwell on a broken heart when you are actively committed to the cause of Christ. If you are brokenhearted and alone, don't wallow in self-pity. Reach out and touch someone. Extend yourself in the service of others. Bring them the gospel. Rejoice with their rejoicing. Weep with their weeping.

Please note that this approach is not just first aid for emergency situations. It is a program for lifelong use. I am always motivated by Paul's epitaph, written to his young protégé Timothy when Paul knew he was near the end of his life:

> For I am already on the point of being sacrificed; the time of my departure has come. I have fought the good fight, I have finished the race, I have kept the faith. Henceforth there is laid up for me the crown of righteousness, which the Lord, the righteous judge, will award me on that Day, and not only to me but also to all who have loved his appearing.
>
> 2 Timothy 4:6–8

Paul stayed actively committed to the cause of Christ right through to the end. He didn't take early retirement at age 55. He didn't just wait to collect his pension. He stayed in the race all the way to the finish line.

This, if I may address a particular word to my older readers, is really the fountain of youth. There are elderly men and women in my church who are among the most active and involved when it comes to reaching out to others. And they have more youthfulness and vitality than many younger people who are already old and jaded because they are so consumed with themselves. These older folks have had a lifetime's worth of struggle and disappointment. Their hearts have been broken, some of them many times over. Paul's heart certainly was. But like Paul they have risen above it because they are still "in the race."

If you want to stay forever young, stay committed to Jesus, committed to the family of Jesus, and committed to the work of Jesus. It is not that you will never have a broken heart. If anything, your heart will be broken all the more as you draw closer to Jesus, because you will be pained with the things that pain him, with the sin and suffering of the whole world. But in Jesus, in his people, and in the great cause of proclaiming his gospel and sharing his love, we have all the healing we need. That is unquenchable hope for the brokenhearted.

Lord Jesus, I thank you that you came to bind up the brokenhearted. I bring to you all the pain and hurt and sorrow of my life. Lord Jesus, I commit my life to you. Thank you for washing away my sin and guilt and for mending my broken heart. I commit myself to your people, my brothers and sisters, to weep with those who weep and to rejoice with those who rejoice, to comfort them and to be comforted by them. I commit myself to your cause: to serving you with joy in the power of your Spirit. Thank you for filling my heart with hope in the midst of a world filled with pain.

7

The Freedom of Forgiveness

Then Peter came up and said to him, "Lord, how often shall my brother sin against me, and I forgive him? As many as seven times?" Jesus said to him, "I do not say to you seven times, but seventy times seven.

"Therefore the kingdom of heaven may be compared to a king who wished to settle accounts with his servants. When he began the reckoning, one was brought to him who owed him ten thousand talents; and as he could not pay, his lord ordered him to be sold, with his wife and children and all that he had, and payment to be made. So the servant fell on his knees, imploring him, 'Lord, have patience with me, and I will pay you everything.' And out of pity for him the lord of that servant released him and forgave him the debt.

But that same servant, as he went out, came upon one of his fellow servants who owed him a hundred denarii; and seizing him by the throat he said, 'Pay what you owe.' So his fellow servant fell down and besought him, 'Have patience with me, and I will pay you.' He refused and went and put him in prison till he should pay the debt.

When his fellow servants saw what had taken place, they were greatly distressed, and they went and reported to their lord all that had taken place. Then his lord summoned him and said to him, 'You wicked servant! I forgave you all that debt because you besought me; and should not you have had mercy on your fellow servant, as I had mercy on you?'

And in anger his lord delivered him to the jailers, till he should pay all his debt.

So also my heavenly Father will do to every one of you, if you do not forgive your brother from your heart."

Matthew 18:21–35

The story is told of a minister who was preaching on Romans 3:23, which tells us that "all have sinned and fall short of the glory of God." He was trying to drive home the point that no one is without sin, and so he challenged his congregation: "Is there anyone here today who is perfect?" He paused a moment for dramatic effect—assuming, of course, that no one would respond to his challenge—and then noticed a man near the back of the church slowly rising to his feet.

The surprised minister called out, somewhat flustered, "Are you perfect, sir?"

"Not me, Reverend," the man replied. "I'm not perfect. I'm standing up for my wife's first husband." Everyone can immediately identify with the poor chap's predicament. We can hear him being nagged day and night by a wife who compares him unfavorably with his dead predecessor. And it is the man at the back of the church who is our counterpart. We know we haven't measured up.

A Double Bind

It is a funny thing about books. As I write these words, I have no idea who will read them. In particular, I know virtually nothing about *you*, who are reading them right now. I don't know where you live or how old you are or what you do for a living. I don't know whether you are married or single or whether you have children. I don't know anything about your personality: whether you are grouchy or pleasant, excitable or placid, joyful or morose.

But there is one thing I do know about you with absolute certainty: I know that you need to be forgiven.

Think about it for just a moment. Is there not some incident in your past, some moment of anger or lust or greed or weakness, in which you gave in to some temptation or another and did something that you now regret? As hard as we try to suppress such memories, to bury them in the backs of our minds, it is a rare person indeed who, if he is honest, is not painfully aware of an action committed or a word said of which he or she is painfully ashamed.

Actually, most of us don't really need to root around in the far corners of our memories to find something for which we need forgiveness. Briefly reviewing the events of the day will do the trick for most of us. When Paul tells us that all have sinned and fallen short of the glory of God, it really doesn't come as news to us. We are all too aware of our need for forgiveness.

By the same token, there is another thing that I know about you with almost the same degree of certainty: There is someone somewhere who needs to be forgiven by you. Someone who has hurt you. Someone who has spoken ill of you. Someone against whom you have been holding a grudge. Again, I am sure you will have no trouble thinking of the person or persons to whom I am referring.

And so each one of us finds himself in a double bind with regard to forgiveness: We need desperately to receive it on the one hand, and we need desperately to grant it on the other. Similarly, we are doubly threatened with regard to unforgiveness. If unforgiveness is shown to us, we are in serious trouble; if unforgiveness characterizes our dealings with others, we are likewise in serious trouble.

Forgiveness: What It Means

Let us take a closer look at how the Bible presents both forgiveness and unforgiveness.

The New Testament has three basic concepts regarding what we call "forgiveness." They are represented by three Greek words, each with a slightly different shade of meaning.

The first and most basic word is *aphiemi*. Strictly speaking it means "to send away," but in its daily usage it had a number of applications. William Barclay outlined them this way:

> It can be used for releasing a man from some sentence that has been passed, as, for instance, from exile. It can be used for remitting a charge that has justly been made. It can be used for acquitting a man from a verdict that might have been carried out or for releasing him from an engagement that might have been insisted upon. It can be used of absolving a man from duty that he could have been compelled to carry out. The whole essence of the word is the undeserved release of a man from something that might justly have been inflicted upon him or extracted from him. Through Jesus Christ man is released from the punishment and penalty that God has every right to inflict upon him. It is the word which tells us that God deals with us, not in justice, but in love; that we are dealt with, not according to our deserts, but according to his mercy and his grace in Jesus Christ. (William Barclay, *New Testament Words* [Philadelphia: The Westminster Press, 1974], p. 125)

Aphiemi is the word used most frequently in the New Testament to mean "forgive." It is, for example, the word that Jesus uses in the Lord's Prayer, teaching us to ask God to "forgive us our debts, as we also have forgiven our debtors" (Matt. 6:12). We can readily see how it applies to God releasing us from a deserved punishment, as Barclay described. We can also see how aptly it describes our forgiving others.

Even though the words "debts" and "debtors" are often passed over as being somewhat old-fashioned, they do nevertheless help us capture the concept of forgiveness. When someone hurts us, we often feel as if they "owe" us some-thing, do we not? How often do we say, speaking of some-one who has caused us pain, "Someday I'll make him pay for that." We really do look upon those who have wronged us as being in some sense our "debtors."

To forgive them, then, means to release them from their debt to us. It means saying, "I'd be justified in making him pay for that, but I won't. Instead I'm going to cancel the debt. He no longer 'owes' me anything."

Tearing Up the IOU

Let's try it. Bring back to mind the person (or one of the persons) you thought of earlier when I talked about people that we need to forgive. One of the most crippling experiences that most people have is holding a grudge, hanging onto a resentment, clutching an emotional IOU against someone somewhere who has done something to hurt us.

Some people hold onto it so long that their lives actually begin to revolve around it. It's like a seed planted in their spirit that takes root and grows and flowers into bitterness and resentment so that it overshadows everything else. It crowds into their thoughts at odd moments, creeps into their conversation, begins to dominate their attitudes to-ward everyone and everything around them.

Whose name and what "debt" are written on the IOU you clutch in your hand? Do you want to be free of the bitter-ness that holding onto that grudge has caused you? Let me tell you what to do. Wherever you are, right now, take a sheet of paper and a pencil and write down the name of the person and what you feel they "owe" you. Take a good look at it. Then, slowly and carefully and deliberately tear up the sheet of paper. Tear it up thoroughly into tiny shreds and then throw the pieces away. As you do all this, in your heart ask God to help you forgive them once and for all. This exercise of "tearing up the IOU" can help us make real the more spiritual process of forgiveness. Any time you are tempted to give in once again to anger or resentment toward that person, remind yourself of the day you definitively tore up the IOU.

Action and Attitude

The second New Testament word for forgiveness is *charizomai*. Some of you will recognize its similarity to the word *charism*, which means gift. *Charizomai* means to grant a favor unconditionally, to act graciously toward another. Jesus used this idea in teaching Peter about forgiveness:

> "A certain creditor had two debtors; one owed five hundred denarii, and the other fifty. When they could not pay, he *forgave* them both. Now which of them will love him more?" Simon answered, "The one, I suppose, to whom he *forgave* more." And he said to him, "You have judged rightly."
>
> Luke 7:41–43

In this story, the *action* entailed in forgiving is described in the same terms as before: releasing someone from a debt. However, it is the *attitude* that is highlighted here. We are not just to be people who forgive, we are to be *forgiving people*, gracious toward others, ready and eager to extend favor or grace to them, especially the grace of forgiveness.

Also implied in this second word is the notion of "paying the cost ourselves." That, of course, is another way of understanding what happens when a debt is remitted. Instead of my demanding that you pay the sum, I decide to bear the cost myself. It would be the same as giving you the money with which to pay me. Thus we see how the idea of "gift" enters into forgiveness.

Let It Pass By

The third word that the New Testament uses for "forgiveness" is *apolyo*. It is used very infrequently in the New Testament, and its precise meaning is difficult to express adequately, but in our context it has the connotation of "letting something pass by."

It is not hard at all to see how this concept relates to forgiveness. How many times a day does someone say or do something that tempts us to react with anger or resentment? How do we respond when such situations arise? Do we pounce on them and immediately write up as big an IOU as possible? Or do we just "let it go," thereby practicing forgiveness?

Let us take it a step further. Do you ever find yourself getting into imaginary conversations with someone? You know what I mean. You see a situation coming in which you *anticipate* (often quite reliably and based on long experience) that someone is *going* to say or do something offensive. And so you begin to live out the experience in advance. *I know just what he's going to say . . . He's going to walk right up to me and say . . . Well, just wait until he does . . . I'm going to turn right around and say to him . . .* Before you know it, your computer is fully programmed. Instead of planning how you are going to let it pass by, you are planning how you are going to latch onto it and milk it for all it's worth.

Jesus teaches us to do just the opposite: to be gracious, to program ourselves to let pass whatever irritating or hurtful things may be approaching. That is the third aspect of biblical forgiveness.

Unforgiveness: A Two-Edged Sword

Having familiarized ourselves with the biblical concept of forgiveness, let's now take a look at what *unforgiveness* looks like. The passage that sums it up best is from the letter to the Hebrews:

> Strive for peace with all men, and for the holiness without which no one will see the Lord. See to it that no one fail to obtain the grace of God; that no "root of bitterness" spring up and cause trouble, and by it the many become defiled.
>
> Hebrews 12:14–15

Let's restate the message of these verses to help bring out their meaning. The passage is basically an exhortation to maintaining good relationships with others: *Strive for peace with all men.* It acknowledges how difficult it is for us to work together in harmony and warns us to be careful lest we begin to relate to one another on some basis other than the love, mercy, and forgiveness that God wants to supply us: *See to it that no one fails to obtain the grace of God.* If we fail to relate to one another with a gracious and forgiving spirit, almost surely a *root of bitterness* will be planted in our hearts. This root of bitterness inevitably *springs up and causes trouble* so that not only we but also other people suffer the consequences.

Let me emphasize that unforgiveness is thus a two-edged sword. The root of bitterness that characterizes unforgiveness is planted *within us.* It is we ourselves, first of all, who suffer when we are unforgiving. We often delude ourselves on this point. We see our refusal to forgive as a weapon against the other person: "There, now," we smugly say to ourselves, "that ought to show *him.*" But in fact we are hurting ourselves as well. Thinking to poison others, we actually wind up poisoning ourselves!

The other edge of the sword is, of course, the effect that our unforgiveness does have on others, not only on the person whom we resent and whom we refuse to forgive but also on all those around us. Unforgiveness not only poisons us, it poisons our whole environment as well.

The Root of Bitterness

Years ago, before I gave my life to the Lord and was called to the ministry, I was studying engineering on a sort of co-op program. I went to school part-time and also worked part-time for a local company. Also working for this company were twin brothers. They had been working together there for many years and had, of course, known each other all their lives. The sad fact was that they never spoke to each other. Never. Not a single word.

Why? Well, at some point in the past, apparently one of them had done something to offend the other, who then presumably returned the offense. Now neither would forgive the other, and things had reached a point where they would not even speak to each other. Whenever a situation arose in which they simply *had* to communicate, they would use another co-worker, a third party, and say, "Go tell my brother thus-and-so."

This was a classic example of a root of bitterness springing up and making life miserable for many. It was clear, for starters, that both of these men were incredibly bitter people. You could almost see the poison of unforgiveness flowing in their veins, souring their whole lives. Moreover, as one of the co-workers who learned to dread being called upon to deliver a third-party message from one of them to the other, I can assure you that everyone around them was made miserable as well. Their bitterness poisoned the whole working environment.

Many of us can provide similar examples from our own experience. I have known wives who harbored unforgiveness toward their husband for something he had done to them years before. Deep within them was a root of bitterness that was poisoning them, their marriage, and their children—all because they would not bring themselves to forgive their husband.

I have known grown men and women who nursed grudges toward their parents for years, believing that their parents had failed them in some way. Now, maybe it was true that their parents *did* fail them. Parents sometimes do fail their children. But ultimately, it was not their parents' failing them that caused them so much pain, it was their own refusal to forgive, to let go of their own bitterness that poisoned their lives and the lives of those around them.

The Poison of Resentment

I have known people—especially men—who have been betrayed in their careers. They gave their lives to the company—"sold their souls to the company store," in the words of an old song—and then were passed over when that once-in-a-lifetime opportunity for promotion came along. As a result they develop a venomous resentment toward their boss, or toward a co-worker who stepped on them, or toward the whole company. From then on, going to work is for them nothing but grief. And they bring that same grief to all who come into contact with them.

Even ministers fall prey to unforgiveness. Shall I let you in on a secret? The pastorate is an extremely painful profession. Consider this: There is no other organization in the world like the church. The product you are working with (the people) is also your boss, your board of directors, and your customer. Think about it. The pastor is working with people who are, in a sense, his product: Their lives are the object of his ministry. They are also, through the church board, his boss. And they are also, in a sense, his customers. They are also his workforce, the fellow laborers who are trained to help produce more mature Christians. This is a very vulnerable position to be in, and many pastors take some very serious blows from it.

I know pastors whose ministries have been destroyed because something has happened to them in their church, and they have not been able to forgive even though they have preached about forgiveness and taught about forgiveness and prayed prayers of forgiveness. A root of bitterness takes hold within them, and before long their ministry suffers, their marriage and family suffers, their whole church suffers. (While I am on this subject, I might add that I have also known churches to suffer because church members have taken offense at their pastor and refused to forgive him in their hearts. So the process works in both directions.)

The Source of Forgiveness

Why am I going to such lengths to point out so many tragic cases? Because I want us to acknowledge the tremendous human and spiritual havoc that is wreaked by unforgiveness. Perhaps one or another of the examples I have cited will strike close to home with you and help you recognize any residue of bitterness that lies at the core of your own unhappiness. If you do recognize a root of bitterness in your heart, the only way to uproot it is through forgiveness. Cancel the debt. Release the obligation. Be gracious and write off the balance due. Tear up the IOU.

Ah, but it's not so easy, you say. Indeed it isn't. In fact, it's so hard that most of us haven't a chance of being able to do it. The root is too firmly planted. We have fed and watered it too long. Pull as hard as we may, we cannot dislodge it.

What are we to do, then? Where are we supposed to get the strength to uproot that root of bitterness? Where do we go to get a supply of forgiveness so that we can give some to someone else?

To Jesus.

That is the lesson I want to draw from the passage from Matthew 18 with which I opened this chapter. Remember? It told of a king who became angry with one of his servants when that servant refused to release one of his fellows from his debt to him. Why did the king get so angry? Why, for that matter, did he expect his servant to be so forgiving toward others? Because the king had already forgiven his servant of a much greater debt. He felt that the servant, having experienced such lavish forgiveness himself, should therefore have been able to extend forgiveness to others.

Obviously, it is not difficult to apply this parable to our own situation. God, the great king, expects us, his servants, to show forgiveness to those around us because he has shown such lavish forgiveness to us. Jesus seems to be saying that to refuse mercy to others when we have been the beneficiaries of such great mercy, is an act of ingratitude on our part.

Moreover, the parable implies that God's forgiveness is the source of our forgiveness. Any time we need to forgive someone else and find it difficult, we are to draw upon the forgiveness that we ourselves have received from God.

Forgiveness and Forgiven-ness

For some of us, this may suddenly shed light on something that we have up until now experienced as a dilemma: We know that we ought to be forgiving people, and we want to extend forgiveness to others, but we find it difficult to do so and we don't know where to turn for help. Could the answer be that we find it difficult to forgive because we ourselves have not experienced forgiveness?

If we are to become forgiving people, it is crucial that we understand and appropriate the magnificent forgiveness that God extends to us in his Son Jesus Christ. Paul explained it in his letter to the Colossians:

> And you, who were dead in trespasses and the uncircumcision of your flesh, God made alive together with him, having forgiven us all our trespasses, having canceled the bond which stood against us with its legal demands; this he set aside, nailing it to the cross.
>
> Colossians 2:13–14

Paul here portrays Jesus as the one who forgives us, the one who models forgiveness for us, and the one who by the power of his forgiveness enables us also to forgive others. He points us to Jesus and says that all our sins—every last one of them—were nailed to the cross, put to death, obliterated, with Jesus.

Let's interpret Paul's image in modern terms. Imagine, if you will, that some sort of cosmic data processing service has been tracking your life since the moment of your birth. It has observed all your actions. It has recorded all your words. It has even been able to transcribe every thought that has passed through your mind. Now imagine that the button is pushed and that this celestial software system begins to produce a computer printout of every sin you have committed.

I don't know about you, but I find that a terrifying thought. A computer printout of all my sins would generate enough paper to cover the walls of several vast cathedrals.

However massive your "printout" might be, take that printout, Paul says, and see it nailed to the cross with Jesus. That is what Jesus has done for us. He has forgiven all our sins. He has paid the just penalty for every single one of them. He has "forgiven us *all* our trespasses, having canceled the bond which stood against us" (in other words, having written off the IOU that God rightly held against us).

The marvelous thing is that once God forgives us, we stay forgiven! God is not as we so often are: He does not just sort of half-heartedly *say* that he forgives us, while continuing to carry a grudge somewhere deep inside.

Once and for All

Isaiah's experience of forgiveness is instructive in this regard: "Thou hast held back my life from the pit of destruction," he says to the Lord, "for thou hast cast all my sins behind thy back" (Isa. 38:17). When God forgives us, he puts our sins out of sight.

The prophet Micah said, "Thou wilt cast all our sins into the depths of the sea" (Micah 7:19). I remember one elderly gentleman back in England who used to quote this verse and say, "He has cast all my sins into the depths of the sea and put a sign on the shore, 'No Fishing Allowed.'"

God's forgiveness is final as far as he is concerned, and he wants it to be final as far as we are concerned, too. We don't need to keep dredging up the memories. We don't need to keep coming to him time after time, burdened with old sins and failings that he has already forgiven, asking him over and over again to forgive them.

"For I will forgive their iniquity," the Lord promised Jeremiah, "and I will remember their sin no more" (Jer. 31:34; see also Heb. 8:12). God puts our sins out of his mind—so much so, in fact, that not even he remembers them! "I am he who blots out your transgressions for my own sake, and I will not remember your sins" (Isa. 43:25). What awesome forgiveness God makes available to us! He puts our sin out of sight, out of reach, out of mind.

Do you need to experience that forgiveness in your own life? You can. Right now, right where you are. Come, as it were, to the cross, bearing the burden of your sins, and hand them over to God to be nailed to the cross with Jesus. Ask God to forgive you for the wrong you have done. Ask him to forgive you for your very unforgiveness, for the pain you have caused others because you would not forgive them. Ask him to lift from your heart the bitterness and resentment you have carried for so long. Ask him to reach down and pull out that "root of bitterness" that has taken hold in your heart. Ask him for the power to be a loving, gracious, forgiving person.

Father, I thank you for sending your Son, Jesus, to die on the cross for me. I now give over to you every sin I have ever committed and ask you to nail it to the cross of Christ. Lift the burden of guilt from my shoulders. Cleanse me of the poison of unforgiveness, and pour through me your love and grace toward those who have wounded me. Lord Jesus, I surrender my life to you. Thank you for bringing me into the freedom of forgiveness.

8

Power to Live in a Defeated World

Every one who believes that Jesus is the Christ is a child of God, and every one who loves the parent loves the child. By this we know that we love the children of God . . . that we keep his command-ments. And his commandments are not burdensome. For whatever is born of God over-comes the world; and this is the victory that overcomes the world, our faith. Who is it that over-comes the world but he who believes that Jesus is the Son of God?

1 John 5:1–5

The church I pastored formerly is located in one of the more fashionable suburbs of Pittsburgh. It is populated, for the most part, by successful and well-to-do people. They live in nice homes, drive nice cars, wear nice clothes.

Their teenage children share in the comfort and affluence that their parents have achieved. They too live in the nice houses and drive the nice cars and wear nice clothes. I think it is safe to say that they would be the envy of a great many teenagers in our country.

But despite the outward appearances, all is not well with these young people. The anguish and frustration that so many of them carry deep within themselves were perhaps reflected best in the tragic experience of one particular young man.

He was fifteen years old, in the same class at high school with one of my own daughters. Several years ago, on the day before school was to resume in the fall, this young man boarded a bus headed for downtown Pittsburgh. But he never arrived there. Somewhere along the route he got off the bus, walked out onto a bridge that spans one of the chasms that surround the city, and jumped off to his death.

He left no suicide note, nor had he given any indication to any of his classmates that anything was wrong. According to my daughter, he was a nice, quiet lad from a good family who did well in school and who seemed, as the old saying goes, to have everything to live for. And yet he took his own life.

This tragedy, occurring as it did so close to home, brought back to my mind an article I had read about a town in Texas, a wealthy suburb of Dallas called Plano.

"The first suicide occurred February 28th," the article states. A boy, sixteen, who was depressed over the death of his friend in a drag race, killed himself. A week later an eighteen-year-old, an "A" student, asphyxiated himself for what his father called "an obsessive need to succeed." Then on April 18 a boy of fourteen, despondent about slipping grades, shot himself. In August a boy and a girl, both seventeen, died together, blaming parental pressure to break up their relationship. Then an eighteen-year-old, distraught over breaking up with his girlfriend, shot himself.

The article then went on to describe how the citizens of Plano were groping for a reason for this veritable epidemic of teenage suicide.

What in the World Is Going On?

Do you ever find yourself frightened and confused as you read the morning paper or watch the evening news on television? We hear about so many bewildering and frightening things: teenage suicide, child abuse, drug-induced death, terrifying sexually-transmitted diseases, divorce, and all the rest. And we are lucky if reading or hearing a news account is as close as we ever come to such things. All too many of us have experienced them in our neighborhoods, among our friends, in our families, even in our own lives. What in the world is going on?

I use the term "world" here quite deliberately. It is one of the most intriguing words in the New Testament. We may be surprised to hear that Scripture has some harsh things to say about "the world":

Do not love the world or the things in the world. If any one loves the world, love for the Father is not in him. For all that is in the world, the lust of the flesh and the lust of the eyes and the pride of life, is not of the Father but is of the world. And the world passes away, and the lust of it; but he who does the will of God abides for ever.

1 John 2:15–17

If the world hates you, know that it has hated me before it hated you. If you were of the world, the world would love its own; but because you are not of the world, but I chose you out of the world, therefore the world hates you.

John 15:18–19

I have manifested thy name to the men whom thou gavest me out of the world; thine they were, and thou gavest them to me, and they have kept thy word. . . . I am praying for them; I am not praying for the world but for those whom thou hast given me, for they are thine.

John 17:6, 9

We know that we are of God, and the whole world is in the power of the evil one.

1 John 5:19

These passages present a sobering, if not shocking, condemnation of the world. If we love it, John says, the love of God cannot be in us, since nothing that is in the world is of the Father. Jesus warns us that the world will hate us just as it has hated him. John finally makes the bold statement that the world is in the very grip of Satan. No wonder we are commanded not to love it!

"The World": Different Meanings

But wait a moment. Are we really to despise the world? And everything in it? Including all the people?

We do well to ask. The Bible uses the word "world" in a number of different senses.

Sometimes when the Bible talks about the world, it means "the whole of the physical creation." In this sense, "the world" is wonderful and, like the heavens, tells of the glory of God. It is his handiwork (Ps. 19:1).

Other times, when the Bible talks about the world, it means "all the people who live in the world." In this sense, too, "the world" is of great value in God's eyes—so much so, in fact, that God sent his only begotten Son, Jesus Christ, to redeem it:

For God so loved the world that he gave his only Son, that whoever believes in him should not perish but have eternal life. For God sent the Son into the world, not to condemn the world, but that the world might be saved through him.

John 3:16–17

So what about the passages we cited earlier that spoke so negatively of "the world"? Clearly, they are using the term to refer to something different. Here is the definition of "the world" in its other, more antagonistic sense: The world is *the system of human society organized apart from God and operating at cross-purposes to him.*

The world and the people who live in it are so valuable to God that he died for them. But there is something else, a system of values and relationships existing within the physical creation and among the people that is at enmity with God and God's plan.

Evangelized into Darkness

This is also the world that tries so hard to draw us to itself, to bring us under its sway—to convert us, if you will, to its way of life. Someone has said that there are two evangelistic programs going on in the universe: God's and Satan's. God's aim is to bring us into his kingdom, a kingdom of light and life and love. Satan's aim is to destroy us in what Scripture calls "the kingdom of the world" (Rev. 11:15), a kingdom of darkness and death and decay.

It is vital for us to realize that we are, at every moment, being evangelized (if one may use the term in this inverted way) into "the world." Advertisements in magazines entice us to greed. Popular songs lure us into lust; some of them—perhaps the young people I described at the beginning of the chapter had listened to them—even glorify suicide and death. The bogus role models presented to us in television programs make us dissatisfied with our lives, our spouses, our careers, our looks, our possessions.

Nor is the campaign limited to the media. We *live* in the midst of "the world." It is part of the air we breathe. Many of the men and women we live near, go to school with, and work with are full-fledged citizens of "the world." Whether intentionally or unintentionally, whether overtly or covertly, they are continually modeling for us and reaffirming in us the ways of thinking, speaking, and acting that characterize life in "the world."

The impact that all this has on us is both subtle and deadly. Subtle because the influence of the world is so pervasive—it is virtually part of the air we breathe—and because it all seems so reasonable, so attractive, so . . . *normal.* Deadly because it steals our affections away from God and prompts us to honor—even to worship—things other than God. And to worship anything other than God can lead only to ruin.

Where Is Your Heart?

Years ago, someone said to me, "If you give your life to anything other than Jesus, it will inevitably destroy you." I have come to see just how true this statement is.

First of all, I have seen it reflected in Scripture. Jesus himself warned us that we could not obey two masters, and that giving our hearts to the things of the world would inescapably choke off our ability to love God (see Matt. 6:24). The apostle John restated this principle when he warned us that "if any one loves the world, love for the Father is not in him" (1 John 2:15).

Paul said much the same thing in his letter to the Romans: "Do you not know that if you yield yourselves to any one as obedient slaves, you are slaves of the one whom you obey, either of sin, which leads to death, or of obedience, which leads to righteousness?" (Rom. 6:16).

However it is expressed, the meaning is the same: To worship anything but God is idolatry, and idolatry leads to futility and death. If you give your life to anything or anyone but Jesus, it will inevitably destroy you.

I have also seen this scriptural principle played out time and time again in the lives of men and women and children. For example, there are men and women who live for their careers, for the money and what it can buy, for the power and prestige that come with title and office.

One of two things happens to such people. They either fail in their pursuit, in which case they become bitter and frustrated, or they succeed, in which case they become strangely disillusioned.

The first group we can readily understand because failure is obviously painful. But have you met people who suffered from success? All their lives they chased a dream. When they finally attained it, they found that it didn't satisfy them after all, and now they have nothing left to live for.

Some parents literally live for their children. Now, on the one hand, they may well bring great blessing to their children because of their devotion. But what happens when the children are all grown up and gone? It is as if God himself had disappeared! I have watched any number of couples spend years trying to find a new center for their lives—and some did not make it because they did not find Christ.

Divorce: The Crushing Weight of the World

Divorce paints one of the most vivid pictures of the impact of "the world" on our lives. All of us are familiar with the appalling divorce statistics. More than half the weddings in our country end in divorce these days, and sadly the percentage seems to be growing.

Have you ever wondered what went wrong in all those marriages? To what are we to attribute this colossal failure rate among marriages? Is it that half of the couples who walked down the aisle actually didn't love each other? Did they set out to have an average marriage? A mediocre marriage? A miserable marriage? Were they saying to themselves, "Well, we'll just go through the motions for a few years and have a couple kids, then we'll get divorced"?

Of course not! They were thinking exactly the same things that everyone thinks when they get married: *Of course we love each other. Of course we're committed to each other. Nothing could ever come between us. Other people have problems, but our marriage is going to be different. We're going to live happily ever after.*

What happened? What went wrong?

The world crushed them.

One of the more challenging tasks that regularly comes my way as pastor of a church is counseling young people who want to be married. There they sit in my office, young, in love, optimistic, a little bit shy. And there I sit, Rev. Wet Blanket, about to intrude upon their romantic reverie with a dose of realism.

Do they know any couples who have been divorced? Yes, of course. Not surprisingly, an increasing number of them are themselves products of a broken home. Do they know any couples *their own age* who have been divorced? Well . . . yes. Do they think those couples planned to fail at marriage? Why, no, of course not. Do they have any idea what went wrong for those couples? Well, not exactly, but, er, that is . . .

In real life, of course, things don't come across quite this bluntly. I wouldn't want to leave you with the impression that my goal is to drive young couples away from marriage. But my goal *is* to awaken them to the challenges that the world poses for them and to the realization that they must make Jesus Christ part of their marriage if they are to have a chance of facing up to those challenges.

Born of God

Here, indeed, is the crucial issue for all of us. How are we going to stand up to the insidious influence of "the world," of this system of human society that is organized apart from God, that operates at cross-purposes to his plan, that is so pervasive, so subtle, so overwhelming?

For whatever is born of God overcomes the world; and this is the victory that overcomes the world, our faith. Who is it that overcomes the world but he who believes that Jesus is the Son of God?

The answer is simple: It is through faith in Jesus Christ that we overcome the world. Jesus himself reassures us in precisely these terms: "In the world you have tribulation; but be of good cheer, I have overcome the world" (John 16:33).

We have already seen the truth of the first part of this statement: Indeed we do have tribulation in the world. And we can readily appreciate our need for some "good cheer" (or, in other words, for encouragement or strengthening); the world is a wily and powerful enemy, fearful in its ability to undermine our strength and courage and to lead us to disaster.

But by his death on the cross, Jesus has put to rout our ancient enemy the devil and has overcome his kingdom, the "kingdom of the world." His victory becomes our victory as we become joined to him.

John expresses the process by which this occurs in a number of ways. We overcome the world by being "born of God," he says. The one who overcomes the world is the one who "believes that Jesus is the Son of God." "Our faith," he explains, is "the victory that overcomes the world."

The famous preacher, Charles Spurgeon, expressed it eloquently:

> Christian, take good care of thy faith; for faith is the only way whereby thou canst obtain blessings. If we want blessings from God, nothing can fetch them down but faith. Prayer cannot draw down answers from God's throne except it be the earnest prayer of the one who believes.
>
> Faith is the angelic messenger between the soul and the Lord Jesus in glory. Let that messenger be withdrawn, and we can neither send up prayer, nor receive the answers.
>
> Take faith away, and in vain I call to God. There is no road between my soul and heaven. Faith links me with divinity. Faith clothes me with the power of God. Faith engages on my side the omnipotence of Jehovah. Faith insures every

attribute of God in my defense. It helps me defy the hosts
of hell. It makes me march triumphant over the necks of my
enemies. Without faith how can I receive anything of the
Lord?

When we commit our lives in faith to the belief that God
sent his Son Jesus to live and die and rise from the dead for
us, Scripture says we are actually adopted into God's family. "To all who received him, who believed in his name, he
gave power to become children of God; who were born, not
of blood nor of the will of the flesh nor of the will of man,
but of God" (John 1:12–13). As John put it in the passage
with which we opened this chapter, *Every one who believes
that Jesus is the Christ is a child of God.*

Power to Become God's Children

Now, many of us have the idea that all men and women,
merely by virtue of their existence, are "children of God."
And I suppose there is a sense in which this is true: We are
part of God's creation, after all, as are the trees and the birds
and everything else he has made. I have heard this general
attitude summarized as "BOM/FOG." The letters stand for
"Brotherhood of Man/Fatherhood of God."

But there really is something foggy about this notion that
all men and women are equally and automatically, by reason of their mere existence, children of God. That certainly
does not seem to be the meaning of the passage from John's
Gospel cited above. It clearly indicates a distinction between
being "born of God" on the one hand and being "born of the
flesh" on the other. It speaks not of our *being* children of
God but of our *becoming* children of God. It says that something must happen to us that enables us to become God's
children: a power that is given, not to everyone, but to those
who "receive" Jesus, who "believe in his name."

It is not until we receive Jesus and believe in him that we
are born of God and thus able to overcome the world.

What about you? Do you find yourself contending with the subtle, vexing, pervasive, overwhelming influence of "the world" in your life? Have you been crushed by its deadening weight? Has your life, your marriage, your family been undermined by its seductive influence? Are you in need of power to live victoriously in the midst of a defeated world?

That is precisely what God has made available to us in his Son Jesus Christ. Power to live in a defeated world. Power to resist temptation. Power to rise above frustration. Power to conquer fear and doubt. Power to overcome death. Power, in short, to become children of God.

How do we get hold of this power? By surrendering our lives to Jesus Christ. By acknowledging that we are sinners in need of forgiveness and that Jesus makes possible that forgiveness through his death on the cross. By committing our lives to be his obedient and joyful servants.

Transformed by God's Love

But how does it work? How does the power of God come into us and work through us, weak creatures that we are, to enable us to overcome the world?

I once heard an account of a mother who took her child to Carnegie Hall to hear the great pianist, Paderewski. During an intermission, the little lad darted away from her in the crowd. As she was threading her way through the lobby trying to find him, she heard a commotion coming from the auditorium. She went back in and was shocked to hear the sounds of "Chopsticks" coming from the grand piano on the Carnegie Hall stage.

Being possessed of that extraordinary "sixth sense" that all parents seem to have, she didn't even have to look to know who it was. Imagine her embarrassment! As quickly as she could, she pushed her way down the main aisle toward the stage to retrieve her son.

She was only halfway there when she suddenly began to hear another sound: some incredibly beautiful music being played along with "Chopsticks." She looked up. There was her son, all right, standing at the piano banging away with his two fingers. But there also was Paderewski himself, standing behind the little boy, reaching around and playing along with him. The child's simple efforts were taken up and transformed by the master, who came and set his hands to the piano.

When we invite Jesus into our lives and the Spirit of God comes to dwell within us, the power of God himself enters our personality and transforms our feeble efforts, turning them into a magnificent symphony—for him.

Does It Really Work?

But does it actually work in practice? Does coming to know Jesus really and truly enable us to overcome the world?

Let me tell you the true story of two people who experienced the overcoming power of God in precisely the area that I described earlier as being most under the attack of the world.

Dave and Elsie had been divorced after several years of marriage. They had two young sons. Dave and Elsie were originally from the Pittsburgh area and married in the church I later pastored.

After the divorce, Elsie ran into a young man she had known years before, who had recently become a Christian. He began to share with her how Jesus had transformed his life. At first, Elsie thought the fellow had lost his marbles. But soon her curiosity got the better of her, and she began attending "her old church" to find out what this "Jesus stuff" was all about. She met more and more people who communicated to her something of the power of God, and before long she too gave her life to the Lord Jesus.

Now Dave was working for a firm headquartered in Chicago, but he spent the weekends in Pittsburgh in order to be with his sons. He immediately began to notice something very different about Elsie. One day he called me on the phone, introduced himself, and asked if we could get together. His ex-wife, the mother of his children, seemed to have gone off the deep end with her religion. Could I offer any insight as to what was going on?

Over breakfast, I explained to him that the changes he saw in Elsie were due to her having given her life to Christ. He seemed willing to accept my explanation—if a bona fide minister thought it was okay, then he guessed he couldn't argue with it—but he wasn't quite so willing to accept Jesus Christ for himself.

Then a remarkable thing happened. A couple of months later Dave was traveling on business. One night, back in his motel room, he switched on the television. There on the screen was a Billy Graham crusade. Normally, Dave would have simply changed channels. But our conversation about Elsie was still in the back of his mind, so he sat down on the bed and listened. When Billy Graham invited the people to come forward and receive Christ, Dave stood up, and there, in his motel room, gave his life to Jesus.

As wonderful as this was, it left Dave and Elsie with a bit of a dilemma. Here they were, newly committed to Jesus, wanting to make a new start in life, divorced from each other, and still suffering from the pain of their divorce. They came to talk to me about the possibility of remarrying but were extremely threatened by the thought of everything going wrong again and then reliving their way through another painful divorce.

My advice to them was to trust in the Lord and, quite simply, start over. Begin courting, I told them. Go back to square one as two single Christians who thought the Lord wanted them to be married. I sent them for counseling to a Christian professional.

One Sunday morning at our 11 o'clock service, before a jam-packed congregation, they committed their lives to one another in marriage—this time in Christ. Since then, they have had two more children. Their marriage is solid and their family is a joy to behold. Dave left his career in business, enrolled in seminary, and today is himself a pastor.

Where does the power come from to work that kind of change in the lives of two badly bruised people? From the Lord Jesus. From faith in his name. From the Holy Spirit whom he, in his great love, sends to live in us when we commit our lives to him. *Who is it that overcomes the world but he who believes that Jesus is the Son of God?*

"They Have Overcome the World"

In the third century, a man named Cyprian was made bishop of Carthage. He was, and still is, renowned for his holiness amid trying times; he was finally beheaded for his faith in Christ. Near the end of his life he wrote a letter to a friend named Donatus that touches upon this matter of overcoming the world. He wrote,

> This seems a cheerful world, Donatus, when I view it from this fair green garden under the shadow of these vines. But if I climb some great mountain and look out over the wide lands, you know very well what I would see. Brigands on the high road; pirates on the seas; in the amphitheatres men murdered to please the applauding crowds; under every roof, misery and selfishness. It is really a bad world, Donatus, an incredibly bad world, yet in the midst of it I have found a quiet and holy people. They have discovered a joy that is a thousand times better than any pleasure of this sinful life. They are despised and persecuted, but they care not. *They have overcome the world.* This people, Donatus, are the Christians, and *I am one of them.*

Are you able to say the same about yourself?

There is in England an ancient Roman city called Chester where there is a wonderful old cathedral with a large clock in the steeple. Around the face of that clock is printed the following meditation:

> When as a child I roamed at will,
>   Time stood still.
> When as a youth I laughed and talked,
>   Time walked.
> When at last I became a man,
>   Time ran.
> Then as I older grew,
>   Time flew.
> Soon I will find while passing on,
>   Time gone. . . .
> Will Christ have saved my soul?

That is the question that each of us must answer. Our life in the defeated world is so brief. One day it will end. The only thing that will matter on that day is the answer to the question on the old clock tower of Chester Cathedral. Will Christ have saved my soul?

You can definitely answer that question right now, right where you are. You can receive Jesus into your heart. You can be born of God and become his child. You can receive from him the power that will enable you to overcome this world and to live with him forever. Pray this prayer:

Lord Jesus Christ, I know that I am a sinner. I believe that you were sent by God to deliver me from my sins and to free me from the power of this sinful world. I believe that you, Jesus, are the Christ, the Son of God, the one sent by God to save the world. I give my life to you now. I promise to follow you as my Lord. Thank you for giving me new life as your child.

9

A Great God Has
a Great Plan for You

For thus says the high and lofty One
  who inhabits eternity, whose name is Holy:
"I dwell in the high and holy place,
  and also with him who is of a contrite and humble spirit,
to revive the spirit of the humble,
  and to revive the heart of the contrite."

Isaiah 57:15

You may recall that I opened this book with the story of a woman who came to me for counseling. She had a great number of very dismaying problems. The thing I was able to say to her that raised her spirits and gave her hope was simply that God loved her and had a wonderful plan for her life.

In the chapters since then we have taken a closer look at the love of God: what it is, and how it makes itself known in our lives. We have looked at a number of the forms in which God expresses his love toward us: by his forgiveness, by making us new creatures, by helping us overcome the world, and so on. Now I would like to go back to the beginning and end where we started with the simple, basic truth that God loves us and has a wonderful plan for our lives. Or, to put it another way, that a great God has a great plan for each of us.

The Eternal God

The place to begin is with a consideration of the greatness of God. The passage from Isaiah with which we opened this chapter says that he is "the high and lofty One who inhabits eternity, whose name is Holy."

Let's talk first about this matter of God "inhabiting eternity." When you hear the word *eternity*, what comes to mind? I think of an experience I have had on several occasions. The first time was several years ago when I was in Colorado for a conference. I was outdoors on the kind of clear night that you only seem to get when you are up in the mountains, the kind of night when the sky is filled with stars. I lay there looking up at the sky and thinking, *I wonder what is beyond the stars?* And the only answer that came to me was, "More stars, I guess." *Well, then, what is beyond those stars?* "Even more stars." *And beyond them?*

Perhaps you have had a similar experience. You begin with an innocent observation and before you know it you have brought yourself face to face with the endlessness, the immensity, the limitlessness of God. And you realize that the universe really does just keep going on and on, far beyond your power to comprehend it, and yet *God fills it all up*. That is one way of grasping the meaning of the phrase, "God inhabits eternity."

But there is much more to the concept of "eternity" than just "endlessness." Eternal life is not just the same mode of life being "stretched out" farther than the eye can see. It is not just more and more of the same thing. It is something qualitatively different, a different dimension of reality. You and I can connect with this dimension now, though only in the most tenuous and incomplete manner. But God *lives* there. He fully and completely inhabits this other dimension of reality that we call "eternity."

All this helps us realize that we will never be able to completely wrap our minds around the full reality of God. We simply cannot do it. God himself tells us so in another passage from Isaiah:

> For my thoughts are not your thoughts,
>   neither are your ways my ways, says the LORD.
> For as the heavens are higher than the earth,
>   so are my ways higher than your ways
>   and my thoughts than your thoughts.
>
> Isaiah 55:8–9

It is a common temptation to hold back from surrendering our lives to God until we *completely* understand him. But that is just another way of saying that we ourselves want to be God. Anyone who could totally comprehend God, who could get his mind and heart to thoroughly surround the knowledge and love of God, would himself have to be greater than God. Surely we know enough to realize that is impossible. God is infinitely greater and vaster than our capacity for comprehension. He is the one who inhabits eternity.

The Holy God

Isaiah tells us not only that God inhabits eternity but also that "his name is Holy." In the Old Testament names were much more than just "labels" or "handles" that you attached to things so that you would have something by which to call them. A name was an expression of a thing's character, its nature, its essence. To say that God's name is Holy is to say that *he is* holy; indeed, it is to say that he is Holiness Itself.

Holiness has two main characteristics. First, it means that God is *whole*, that he is purely and perfectly of one nature and one character. Do you know how we sometimes speak of other people as "having it all together"? Well, God has it all together. He is utterly integrated. He is not splintered, not fragmented, not scattered all over the place. He is not one thing one minute and another thing the next minute. God is altogether the same God all the time.

The Bible says it this way: God is "the Father of lights with whom there is no variation or shadow due to change" (James 1:17). Another rendering has it that in God "there is no shadow cast by his turning." This image communicates something of the other perfection of God. If the presence of God could cast a shadow, the shape would be perfectly uniform, like a turning sphere that shows no irregularities in its shadow.

Again, we are using a woefully inadequate image to describe something that is ultimately indescribable. The point is simply that God is totally integrated. He will never look different one day than he did the day before. He is utterly at one with himself.

Moreover, because he is thus integrated, he acts with complete integrity. He never acts in a way that is at variance with who he is. He is always true to himself. Or as Paul put it, even "if we are faithless, he remains faithful—for he cannot deny himself" (2 Tim. 2:13).

God Outside the System

Holiness also means that God is separate from us. The Scriptures sometimes portray this in terms of actual physical separation: He is "the high and lofty One" who "dwells in the high and holy place" (Isa. 57:15).

But there is more to God's "separateness" than mere altitude. God is totally and completely *other than* everything that we humans are or can even conceive. He is not just "man-and-woman" in some modified, exalted form. He is not just the product of human imagination. He is, to use a term from the philosophers, "wholly other."

This is one of the great dividing points between Christianity and the various Eastern religions. They are unable to conceive of a God who is a real person, an individual with whom they can have a real relationship. Rather they see God as the sum total of all creation. Thus they say that God is in me and in you, that God is in nature, that God is in the trees, in the air, in the buildings, in my shoes and socks (I suppose—where, after all, is one to draw the line with this way of thinking?).

This is not the Judeo-Christian understanding. We know God to be totally and completely apart from and independent of ourselves. He is not dependent on us for his existence. If the entire creation were to disappear into nothingness, the Eastern "God" would simply disappear into nothingness right along with it. Biblical teaching bears more relationship to objective reality as we know it. God addresses us, as it were, from "outside the system." From the Bible's point of view, if the whole of creation should cease to exist, God would remain intact, not in the least diminished.

God Within Us

And yet address us he does. That is the amazing thing. This God who is totally "other," utterly holy, who inhabits eternity and never changes, this God who is high and lofty and who dwells in the high and holy place, also seeks to make his home within you and me. "I dwell in the high and holy place," he says, "and also with him who is of a contrite and humble spirit, to revive the spirit of the humble, and to revive the heart of the contrite." He dwells in the heavens, and he also wants to dwell in our hearts. Why? Because his greatness is not impersonal. Our God is so great that for all his immensity he loves each of us personally.

What is more, it is *he* who comes to *us*. We are always trying to "be good," as if by so doing we could somehow merit his attention and his love. But we can never do it. We can never come to God or get him to come to us on our terms. We cannot negotiate with him, as though we could somehow split the difference between his interests and our own.

No, it must always be on his terms. And his terms are that he will come to dwell in the man or woman who has a contrite and humble spirit. This is another description of our need to be dependent on God and to yield our hearts to him. Contrition is deep remorse at our willful self-centered rejection of him and his ways which the Bible calls sin. Humility is yielding our hearts to God and *his estimate* of the way things really are in our lives.

Who Chooses Whom?

All this adds up to a simple truth that is repeated frequently in the Bible: God chooses us. He is the creator and initiator of the relationship between himself and his people. Our choice of him is meaningful only because it comes in response to his initiative. We have already seen how John makes this point. "In this is love, not that we loved God but that he loved us and sent his Son to be the expiation for our sins. . . . We love, because he first loved us" (1 John 4:10, 19). Paul says much the same thing in his first letter to the Thessalonians: "For we know, brethren beloved by God, that he has chosen you" (1 Thess. 1:4). And, of course, Jesus himself says it as explicitly as it can possibly be said: "You did not choose me, but I chose you and appointed you that you should go and bear fruit and that your fruit should abide" (John 15:16).

One of the images that the New Testament often uses to describe our relationship to God is that of adoption:

> When the time had fully come, God sent forth his Son, born of woman, born under the law, to redeem those who were under the law, *so that we might receive adoption* as sons. And because you are sons, God has sent the Spirit of his

Son into our hearts, crying, "Abba! Father!" So through God you are no longer a slave but a son, and if a son then an heir.

Galatians 4:4–7

Notice that even this idea of adoption carries with it the notion of God choosing us, selecting us. Adoption involves a process of selection. It was not that many years ago that when you wanted to adopt a baby, there were many to choose from. You could, figuratively if not literally, walk down the row and pick out the baby you wanted to adopt. We can bring that notion into our understanding of what it means to say that God adopts us. He picks us out. He points right at us and says, "I'd like that one to be my son. I'd like that one for my own daughter."

Part of the Master's Plan

Why does he choose us? Because he loves us, of course. But I think we can carry it one step further. He chooses us, he "picks us out," because he has a plan for us, because he sees what we can become through his grace, because he sees how we in particular can be fruitful in his service.

Try to imagine it being otherwise. Imagine that right this very moment you decide to surrender your life to Christ, to respond to God's choosing of you by choosing him in return. What do you think our heavenly Father is going to do next? Picture him sitting there, scratching his head, glancing over at the Son and saying, "Whatever are we going to do with this one? Well, now, here she is. I really haven't the foggiest notion myself."

Then picture Jesus turning to the Holy Spirit and saying, "I don't know. What do you think? Have you any use for her?"

And now picture the Holy Spirit turning to the Father and the Son and saying, "Well, I'm not sure. Let's just wait and see. Who knows how she might develop? We'll keep an eye on her, and if she turns out to be suitable for something or other, we'll see if we can slip her in someplace."

It is clear that the very idea of this divine indecision is absurd. When we come to the Lord he knows *exactly* what he intends to do with us. His plan is absolutely clear in his mind. Indeed, it has been clear right from the beginning. He has only been looking for that moment when we respond to him so that he can begin to implement it in our lives. Listen to how God describes this very thing in terms of the prophet Jeremiah:

Now the word of the Lord came to me saying,

"Before I formed you in the womb I knew you,
and before you were born I consecrated you;
I appointed you a prophet to the nations."

Then I said, "Ah, Lord God! Behold, I do not know how to speak, for I am only a youth." But the Lord said to me,

"Do not say, 'I am only a youth';
for to all to whom I send you you shall go,
and whatever I command you you shall speak.
Be not afraid of them,
for I am with you to deliver you,

says the Lord."
Jeremiah 1:4–8

What phenomenal reassurance to know that God had a purpose in mind for each one of us even since before we were born! Jeremiah's call was to be a prophet. The precise calling will of course be different for each of us, but the basic fact remains the same—God has had a loving plan in mind for our lives since the very beginning of our existence.

Excuses, Excuses

And many of us are making exactly the same kind of response to God that Jeremiah made. "Ah, Lord God," he moans. "That plan will never work for me, I can't speak very well. And besides, I'm too young."

What is your excuse? What reason do you have for why you cannot do whatever it is God has called you to do? Do you think you are too young? This particular line of excuse follows an interesting pattern.

The high school student thinks to himself, "I'm too young to do anything for God. Just wait until I get to college, away from home and my parents."

The college student says, "I'm too young to do anything significant for God. Just wait until I graduate, and get out there in the real world with a job and a car and a place of my own."

The young married couple says, "We can't be of any use to God. We're just starting out. We're all caught up in buying a house and starting a family and launching a career. Just wait until we get established."

A few years later the same couple says, "Teenagers! How are we ever going to be able to do anything worthwhile for God until we get these teenagers squared away and off to college?"

And do you know what that same couple says once the teenagers *do* go off to college and then graduate? "We're exhausted. Now that the kids are off our hands we owe ourselves time to relax." We're never going to get anywhere with God by focusing on the limitations of our age or circumstances.

How about Jeremiah's other excuse? "Behold," he said, "I do not know how to speak." How often do we "beg off" from serving God because we think we lack the requisite gifts and talents? This, too, is rather foolish. After all, God has already said to Jeremiah that it was he who had formed

Jeremiah in the womb. He "put Jeremiah together," so to speak. He knew, far better than Jeremiah knew, what Jeremiah was and was not equipped to do.

No Accidents

So it is with us as well. God's plan for our life is never separated from God's provision for our life. He never appoints us to do anything he has not or will not equip us to do.

In a sense, what Jeremiah was really saying to God was, "I can't do it. I'm nothing. I'm nobody. *You've made a mistake.*"

What an insult to God! To say to him, "Lord, you loved me enough to create me and to put me together exactly the way you wanted me, and your Son Jesus loved me enough to die on the cross for me so I could be restored to friendship with you, and your Holy Spirit loves me enough to dwell inside me and give me your power—but I'm a nobody. I'm useless. You're making a big mistake in calling me into your service." How could anyone for whom the great, mighty, eternal, holy God has done so much be a nobody?

Let us clear our minds of this kind of thinking. The fact is that the Lord *formed* us in the womb. He *has* called us to himself, redeemed us from our sin, empowered us by his Spirit, and equipped us to serve him, because he *does* love us and because he *does* have a wonderful plan for our lives. Paul sums it up in a line from his letter to the Ephesians: "For we are his workmanship, created in Christ Jesus for good works, which God prepared beforehand, that we should walk in them" (Eph. 2:10).

We are not "cosmic accidents," we are God's workmanship. When Jesus died for us, he knew what he was doing. When he drew us to faith in himself, he knew who he was winning. He knows what he has in mind for us—and it has all been conceived and worked out in his love.

"Just for Me"

Our theme in this chapter has been that there is a great God who has a great plan for us. We have talked about the greatness of God, and we have talked about what it means that he has a plan. Now we must conclude by reminding ourselves that this great God has a great plan for *us*.

Jesus told a parable that expressed the intensely personal and individual concern God has for us:

> What do you think? If a man has a hundred sheep, and one of them has gone astray, does he not leave the ninety-nine on the mountains and go in search of the one that went astray? And if he finds it, truly, I say to you, he rejoices over it more than over the ninety-nine that never went astray. So it is not the will of my Father who is in heaven that one of these little ones should perish.
>
> Matthew 18:12–14

The crucial thing to bear in mind is that you—you who are at this very moment reading these words on this page—are that one sheep. It is you, personally, whom Jesus has gone out to find. It is you he wants to bring home. It is you for whom our great God has a great plan.

Do you realize this? Is it part of the way you think about God's love for you? It made an enormous impact on me the first time I heard it. The man who was sharing the gospel with me told me that even if I, John Guest, had been the only person who had ever sinned and needed a Savior, Jesus would have gone to the cross and died *just for me.*

I think that most of us, without quite realizing it, see things a bit differently. We see Jesus coming to die for the sins of "the whole world," for the mass of humanity down through history, and thus coming to die for us only in the sense that we happen to belong to the whole of "humanity." That is true in its own way, but it totally misses the intensely personal element of God's love for us.

In the French language there are two words for the personal pronoun "you." There is *vous*, which refers to a group of people and has a somewhat formal, impersonal ring to it, and *tu*, which refers to a single individual and implies a closeness and intimacy that is lacking in *vous*. When God says, "I love you," he means it in both ways. He loves all of us, and he loves each of us. Each and every one of us can say, "God loves us" and "God loves *me*."

The Empty Chair at the Table

They had just taken their son off to college. Here is how the father described it to a friend he was hoping to introduce to Jesus:

> Nearly a year ago Peg and I
> had a very hard week.
> Wednesday night—
> Mike slept downstairs in his room—
> where children belong
> and we slept upstairs in ours
> where moms and dads belong.
> Thursday night—
> we were 350 miles away and he was
> in Ramada 325 and we were in 323—
> connecting rooms and we left the door open
> and talked and laughed together.
> Friday night—
> 700 miles from home and
> he was in 247 and we were in 239
> but it was just down the balcony
> and somehow we seemed together.
> Saturday night—
> he was in the freshman dorm
> and we were still in 239.
> Sunday night—
> we were home and he was
> 700 miles away in Chapman 309.

Now we have been through this before
Bob Jr. had gone away to college
and we had gathered ourselves together
until we had gotten over it—
mainly because he's married now
and he only lives ten miles away
and comes to visit often
with Deb and Robert the III.
So we thought we knew
how to handle separation pretty well
but we came away so lonely and blue.

Oh our hearts were filled with pride
at a fine young man
and our minds were filled with memories
from tricycles to commencements
but deep down inside somewhere
we just ached with loneliness and pain.

Somebody said you still have three at home—
three fine kids and there is
still plenty of noise—
plenty of ball games to go to—
plenty of responsibilities—
plenty of laughter—
plenty of everything . . .
except Mike
And in parental math
five minus one
just doesn't equal plenty.

And I was thinking about God
He sure has plenty of children—
plenty of artists,
plenty of singers,
and carpenters,
and candlestick makers,
and preachers,
plenty of everybody . . .

except you
and all of them together
can never take your place.
And there will always be
an empty spot in His heart—
and a vacant chair at His table
when you're not home.

And if once in a while
it seems He's crowding you a bit—
try to forgive Him.
It may be one of those nights
when He misses you so much
He can hardly stand it.

God Longs for You

Perhaps you have been feeling God "crowd" you a little as you have read this book. That is nothing more than God trying to tell you that he loves you, he really wants you to respond to him and come home.

And respond you must. Jesus didn't die for you just because he died for everybody and you're part of "everybody." He died on the cross as if you were the only one who needed salvation. And that, conversely, is just how you need to respond to him. You can't squeeze in with the crowd. You won't be able to come shuffling down the lane with the great mass of humanity and duck in with everyone else. God's initiative has been made to you personally and individually, and your response must also be personal and individual.

I'm going to end this book by doing something I've already done several times: invite you to give your life to Jesus Christ. You may be on a plane. You may be sitting up in bed. It is possible for you, wherever you are right now, to come to Jesus. He loves you as much right now as he did the moment he died on the cross for you. He couldn't love you any more. He longs for you to know that love, to receive it, to respond to it. He longs to forgive the wrong you have done. He longs to make you a new person, to unfold his perfect plan for your life, to heal your broken heart, to empower you to rise above the defeated world around you. He longs for *you*.

He is calling out to you, inviting you to come to him. Will you answer his call?

Dear Lord Jesus, I have been away from you far too long. Thank you for patiently pursuing me. Right now I want to stop running away. I turn around and yield myself to you. Come into my life, Lord Jesus. Forgive me of all that is past. Fill me with yourself. Fill me with your forgiveness. Fill me with your power. As far as I am able, I give myself to you. Fulfill your plan for my life.

Thank you, Heavenly Father, for this wonderful gift, through Jesus Christ, my Lord. Amen.